RESOLUTE

RESOLUTE

An Unwavering Stance on the Truth of God's Word

DAVID SHELDON
KERRI SHELDON

Published by 4 Truth Ministry
Mansfield, Ohio
4truthministry.com

Printed by CreateSpace
Available from Amazon.com and other online stores

Sheldon, David, 1950-
Sheldon, Kerri, 1981-
Resolute: an unwavering stance on the truth of God's Word / David Sheldon / Kerri Sheldon.

ISBN-13: 978-0-9906018-0-7
1. Resolute – Religion – Christianity. 2. Evangelicalism. 3. Christian Life.

DEDICATION

To "The Great Shepherd of the sheep…Jesus our Lord."
(Hebrews 13:20)

THANK YOU

We would like to thank all who prayed for us during the writing of this book. Special thanks to the following for their prayer and input:

Lynn Sheldon
Tammi Wright
Craig, Amy, Allison, & Andrew Redmond
Erin Benziger (donotbesurprised.com)

ABOUT 4 TRUTH MINISTRY

4 Truth Ministry is a Christian teaching ministry that seeks to help Christians grow in their knowledge of God through His Word. Currently, fundamental Scriptural truths are being ignored or displaced. In response, we proclaim and defend truth. Please visit www.4truthministry.com for more information.

CONTENTS

INTRODUCTION

Children are often times told to hold the hand of a parent. It is because they tend to wander, and a parent's hand will guide and protect them. While the parent typically maintains the grip, the child is still told to grab on. Similarly, Christians need guidance in their Christian walk. God has provided Scripture as His hand of direction and protection. Charles Spurgeon stated, "Happy are we to have God's Word always to guide us! What were the mariner without his compass? And what were the Christian without the Bible?"[1]

Is today's Christian culture, as a whole, holding onto God's Word as its only guide? To find out, this book asks questions regarding certain popular topics such as:

1. Hearing God's Voice - Does God have more to say?
2. Experiencing God - How does God "come" to us?
3. Telling "Your" Story - Can God's story be your story?

The first question addresses the nature of God's revelation and whether or not it is complete. The second question identifies how God makes Himself known and if God's Word was and is sufficient. The third question pinpoints if, in people telling their story of God's salvation, the content and characters are being kept in their proper context. The conglomeration of thought surrounding these areas helps us gauge if visible Christianity is retaining the standard of God's Word as Paul said to do:

> Retain the standard of sound words which you have heard from me, in the faith and love which are in Christ Jesus. (2 Timothy 1:13) (All Scripture quoted herein are NASB version unless noted otherwise.)

In looking at the history of the church, there is evidence of the infiltration of false teachings. To remain pure, the church put up great fights to clarify the truth and do away with the false. Today is no different. Christians must evaluate all teachings according to Scripture—even those labeled "Christian." When they do not line up, we must clearly avoid them and carefully bring truth to bear.

As we will see, when wholesome preaching and teaching of God's Word is compromised, a resulting theological mixture can become a standard of its own.

Paradoxically, the presence of both false teaching and deception are a part of God's plan, especially at the end of the age. Various passages in 2 Thessalonians and Revelation speak to this reality. We will examine certain texts and give thoughtful consideration to each, encouraging Christians to remain faithful to God and His Word at all times.

1

THINK ABOUT IT

...my conscience is captive to the Word of God...[1]

—Martin Luther

Imagine you are on a trip with other members of your church congregation. The leader, whom you all trust, is at the wheel of the bus. Time is flying as you enjoy the company and the music. A pause in conversation allows you to stretch back and glance out the window. You see a road sign that reads, "Exit 153: Begin Your Adventure with Jesus." As the bus slows down you see more signs, "Turn Right: Engage in Your Spiritual Journey" and "Enter: God's Story Can Be Your Story."

Somewhat confused, you can't help but wonder exactly where you are going. Within seconds, the radio DJ comes on and announces, "Listener, if God had a wallet, your picture would be in it. Next on the play list: It's all about Him and He's all about you."

Now you are completely bewildered. It seems what you just read and heard was intended to resemble Christianity, but an underlying current of self-interest and self-satisfaction is undeniably present. The real call to know and follow Christ—the call of discipleship—is one of repentance and self-denial:

> Then Jesus said to His disciples, "If anyone wishes to come after Me, he must deny himself, and take up his cross and follow Me. For whoever wishes to save his life will lose it; but whoever loses his life for My sake will find it. (Matthew 16: 24-25)

Scratching your head, you look across the seats. No one else appears to be bothered. You lean over to ask, "Did you see the signs out there?"

"Oh, I think so. What's wrong with them? Are you concerned about something? The leader has assured us he knows where he is going, so why should we worry? I'm sure we'll be fine."

On the other hand, you know full well Scripture does not offer such nebulous appeals or mandates. You sink back in your seat knowing you didn't sign up for this. To you, traveling in the Christian bus meant you were on board with the way it was going. But this can't possibly be the right direction. Should people place blind trust in anything or anyone labeled Christian?

....

Obviously the above scenario is made-up, but it metaphorically speaks of a "Christian" religion surrounded by callings different than the calling found in Scripture.

The calling found in Scripture is one of faith in Christ.

God's gospel message is simple and clear: Christ died on the cross for our sins, was buried, and rose again, as Lord and Savior. It is that message that saves and calls people to know and follow Christ. Being a disciple of His includes repentance and self-denial and demands up front that a price is going to have to be paid.

The appeals in our scenario, similar to ones we often hear today, are not only unclear, but they could in fact call someone to a life of ease and self-fulfillment. It is no wonder they are so popular.

But why would contrived calls, not based solely in truth, stand as the current "Christian" road map? We will view, in light of Scripture, popular topics such as hearing God's voice, experiencing God, and telling "your" story. Doing this will help us decipher the accuracy of many current teachings.

2

HEARING GOD'S VOICE

If your imaginary revelation is not according to this Word, it has no weight with us; and if it is according to this Word, it is no new thing. Brethren, this Bible is enough if the Lord does but use it and quicken it by his Spirit in our hearts. Truth is neither your opinion, nor mine; your message, nor mine. Jesus says, 'Thy word is truth.' That which sanctifies men is not only truth, but it is the particular truth which is revealed in God's Word—'Thy word is truth.' What a blessing it is that all the truth that is necessary to sanctify us is revealed in the Word of God, so that we have not to expend our energies upon discovering truth, but may, to our far greater profit, use revealed truth for its divine ends and purposes! There will be no more revelations; no more are needed.[1]

—Charles Spurgeon

God's Word is only, and never more than, the canon of Scripture. He breathed out His revealed truth one time, making the Scriptures fixed, complete, and sufficient. Charles Spurgeon recognized this when he unwaveringly stated that sanctifying truth is found only in Scripture and any claims otherwise can be ignored.

There is a common belief in our day that God speaks truth

to people in addition to Scripture whether internally or externally through visions, dreams, impressions, prods or other people. This notion brings us to the first main question "Does God have more to say?" That is, did God leave room beyond the Scripture to personally and directly speak to people today?

Some think God directly speaks to people today because He directly spoke to people in biblical times. A prime example is found in Henry and Richard Blackaby's book *Hearing God's Voice* when they wrote:

> The question, then, is not *whether* God speaks to His people, but *how*? Perhaps you have been confused about what God is saying to you...If you have not heard God speak to you, perhaps you have come to assume your experience is normative for the Christian life. This book is written to help you clearly recognize God's voice. When God speaks, He does not give new revelation about Himself that contradicts what He has already revealed in Scripture. Rather, God speaks to give application to His Word of the specific circumstances in your life. When God speaks to you, He is not writing a new book of Scripture, rather, He is applying to your life what He has already said in His Word.[2]
>
> Does God speak to people today?...Even a casual perusal of the Bible reveals a consistent pattern of God speaking to people.[3]

The Blackabys say God revealed Himself in Scripture, and they also say He speaks to give application of that Scripture. Think about that. Does God actually *speak* application of His Word? Or, in reading Scripture, are our minds renewed with the truth so that we can walk by faith according to that truth? The later, of course, is accurate.

So yes, God spoke His Word, but we do not need to wait to hear Him speak the application of it or in addition to it. Let's now look more closely at Scripture to find out why and how God spoke in the past and if He directly speaks to people today.

REVELATION GIVEN

God has made Himself known. This is called His revelation. Louis Berkhof, former professor at Calvin Seminary in Grand Rapids, Michigan, gave a working definition of God's revelation:

> And when we speak of revelation, we use the term in the strict sense of the word. It is not something in which God is passive, a mere "becoming manifest," but something in which He is actively making Himself known. It is not, as many moderns would have it, a deep and spiritual insight which leads to an ever increasing discovery of God on the part of man; but a supernatural act of self-communication, a purposeful act on the part of the Living God. There is nothing surprising in the fact that God can be known only if, and insofar as, He reveals Himself.
>
> Without revelation man would never have been able to acquire any knowledge of God. And even after God has revealed Himself objectively, it is not human reason that discovers God, but it is God who discloses Himself to the eye of faith.[4]

At times, God's self-disclosure involved Him appearing (theophany) such as when He came to Moses in the burning bush in Exodus 3. Moses, though fascinated with what he saw, did not understand it was God he was seeing. God verbally spoke from the bush for Moses to understand. At other times, God disclosed Himself without making an appearance at all. This is seen repeatedly throughout the Old Testament when it says, "The Word of the Lord came to..." His Word was and is His self-revealed thoughts as Paul explains in 1 Corinthians 2:

> For to us God revealed *them* through the Spirit; for the Spirit searches all things, even the depths of God. For who among men knows the *thoughts* of a man except the spirit of the man which

is in him? Even so the *thoughts* of God no one knows except the Spirit of God. Now we have received, not the spirit of the world, but the Spirit who is from God, so that we may know the things freely given to us by God, which things we also speak, not in words taught by human wisdom, but in those taught by the Spirit, combining spiritual *thoughts* with spiritual *words*. (1 Corinthians 2:10-13)

Further, God revealed His very person in the Incarnate Jesus Christ:

In the beginning was the Word, and the Word was with God, and the Word was God...And the Word became flesh, and dwelt among us, and we saw His glory, glory as of the only begotten from the Father, full of grace and truth. (John 1:1, 14)

Jesus Christ was and is God's final revelation of Himself to this present age until Christ returns in glory:

God, after He spoke long ago to the fathers in the prophets in many portions and in many ways, in these last days has spoken to us in His Son, whom He appointed heir of all things, through whom also He made the world. (Hebrews 1:1-2)

All of God's revealed thoughts are the words of truth we find in Scripture (Psalm 119:160). That revelation was and is perfect and complete.

REVELATION CIRCULATED

It is critical to remember that God did not reveal truth all at one time, nor was it written down all at one time. Truth was revealed by God over a period of time, and then, for the most part, it was passed along verbally before it was all written down.

The revelations of God during the early church were given to apostles and prophets and passed along verbally before they were written down. They were perfectly given from God to His chosen authorities. But then what happened? They were passed along to elders and other believers. After having thought about this reality, consider what Paul says:

> Do you not remember that while I was still with you, I was telling you these things? (2 Thessalonians 2:5)

Paul reminds the Thessalonians of the revelatory truths he had only spoken to them before! And further:

> So then, brethren, stand firm and hold to the traditions which you were taught, whether by word *of mouth* or by letter from us. (2 Thessalonians 2:15)

> The things which you have heard from me in the presence of many witnesses, entrust these to faithful men who will be able to teach others also. (2 Timothy 2:2)

The truths we now know as the words of prophetic Scripture for the most part were first delivered verbally. Those in New Testament times lived after Christ ascended and before the completion of Scripture. Consider the sequence of truths from verbal form to the final written form:

— For approximately the first 18 years of the church's existence, 33-50 A.D., Christians only had the written Old Testament.
— During those 18 years, truth regarding the person of Christ and His earthly ministry existed in the form of authoritative speech.
— The Holy Spirit revealed truth incrementally to those He had designated for the task. As they received further revelation, just like Jesus had told them

9

would happen, the apostles and prophets faithfully passed it along verbally.

— The primacy of apostolic authority was clearly evident.

— As elders/pastors were appointed to the various churches, they faithfully taught the things the apostles and prophets had verbally taught them.

— Because of no written authority, false teachers took advantage and entered the church with their teachings. Confusion as to what was and was not authoritative teaching was very possible.

— Then, approximately 50 A.D., the New Testament started being written. So in addition to authoritative speech, there were some authoritative writings. It took quite some time for these writings to be copied and circulated.

— Eventually the Scripture was finalized with John's book of Revelation in approximately 95 A.D.

This progression from verbal truth to written Scripture is evident in Paul's teachings. In his early letters—Thessalonians and Corinthians—Paul gives instruction regarding the role of prophets and the gift of prophecy. The church, in its infancy, received instruction from Paul as to revelations, prophetic utterances, and the gift of prophecy. In the middle of his ministry—Ephesians—he writes that the office of apostles and prophets is foundational (Ephesians 2:20). They were God's firmly established authoritative spokespersons. Then, in Paul's last two letters, 1 & 2 Timothy, he instructs Pastor Timothy to faithfully preach and teach the Word of God. No wonder in Paul's early ministry he said the following:

Do not quench the Spirit; do not despise prophetic utterances. But examine everything *carefully*; hold fast to that which is good; abstain from every form of evil. (1 Thessalonians 5:19-22)

Paul tells the Thessalonians to not despise prophetic utterances because they were not to disregard verbal truth! Prophetic utterances were the only means of people knowing truth concerning the Savior. As prophetic utterances were being written down, the emphasis shifted from truth being in verbal form to truth being in the form of written Scripture.

In summary, God spoke in a progressive manner and during a time of transition before the Scripture was completed. This is the "how" of God's spoken self-revelation.

IS THERE MODERN DAY PROPHECY?

Historically, there have been two categories of prophecy.

- *First Category Prophecy* is revelation found in the Old Testament. It was the Word of God delivered by various means and written down with no error. It is complete and perfect.
- *Second Category Prophecy* is revelation found in the New Testament. It was the Word of God spoken/written down with no error. It is complete and perfect.

Recently, another category has been introduced titled Third Category Prophecy:

- *Third Category Prophecy* is defined as revelation which operated in the New Testament church along with Second Category Prophecy. It supposedly continues in operation today while Second Category has ceased. It is considered a kind of prophecy not authoritative in nature in that it is the receiving of an impression by the Holy Spirit. It is beyond the canon of Scripture. It is not so complete and not so perfect!

Third Category Prophecy was popularized by Wayne Grudem in his book *The Gift of Prophecy in the New Testament and Today*[5] and is supported by John Piper on his Desiring God website.[6] Together they have affirmed its concept as theologically sound. These prophecies are said to be of another category than the first two because they were not "universal truth" or truth applicable to everyone, and thus did not carry the same authoritative weight.

According to Third Category teaching, God gave individual revelation to people of the New Testament church. It was given for a particular occasion or for personal direction. But if these personal revelations were not authoritative enough to be included in the canon, were they of a sure foundation? That is, were they actually of God and part of His revelation of truth?

Dr. John MacArthur, teacher at Grace to You and pastor at Grace Community Church in Sun Valley, California, addresses the topic:

> John's [Piper] view is also Wayne Grudem's view, and represents a radical departure from the historic position of the Christian church. More to the point, it is a direct contradiction of 2 Peter 1:21: "No prophecy was ever made by an act of human will, but men moved by the Holy Spirit spoke from God."...From Genesis to Revelation, the Bible demonstrates four foundational characteristics of true prophecy. First, true prophecy is always verbal, the very words of God. It's never an impulse or an impression; it's never a feeling that needs interpretation... Second, true prophecy is propositional—it is testable as either true or false...Third, true prophecy is infallible. Whatever God spoke through His prophets was error-free and utterly unaffected by human fallibility. Fourth, because a true prophecy is verbal, propositional, and inerrant, the only conclusion to draw is that it carries the full weight of divine authority. Ever since the end of the apostolic age and the completion of the canon, only Scripture can legitimately claim that level of authority (2 Timothy 3:16).[7]

In actuality, supposed Spirit-given personal revelations were not included in the canon because there was no such thing. God breathed out His revelatory Word one time. His Spirit does not speak beyond that. All prophetic truth was already delivered, and it can be found in the written Scripture.

When all revealed truth was written down, the canon of Scripture was complete. His truth is now imparted to us only on the pages of Scripture. As John Calvin said, "God bestows the actual knowledge of Himself upon us only in the Scriptures."[8]

The Westminster Confession of Faith, an all-encompassing religious document written in 1646 by an assembly of 121 Puritan clergymen, emphasized the sufficiency of Scripture very concisely and pointedly:

> The whole counsel of God, concerning all things necessary for his own glory, man's salvation, faith, and life, is either expressly set down in Scripture, or by good and necessary consequence may be deduced from Scripture: unto which nothing at any time is to be added, whether by new revelations of the Spirit, or traditions of men. Nevertheless we acknowledge the inward illumination of the Spirit of God to be necessary for the saving understanding of such things as are revealed in the Word...[9]

Our own opinions and judgments are not God's Word and should be set aside while reading and interpreting it. Luther said it well:

> What is asserted without the Scriptures or proven revelation may be held as an opinion, but need not be believed.[10]
> What kind of God would He be if His Word, being insufficient, were in need of a supplement from men?[11]

If we need help understanding it, we should look at other Scripture. William Gurnall wrote about this in his book *The Christian in Complete Armor:*

> The best way therefore to know the mind of God in one text, is to lay it to another. The lapidary uses one diamond to cut another; so should we use one place of Scripture to interpret another. Scriptures compared, like glasses set one against another, cast a light each to the other.[12]

God takes the finality of His Word very seriously. There are dire consequences for anyone who tampers with it:

> I testify to everyone who hears the words of the prophecy of this book; if anyone adds to them, God will add to him the plagues which are written in this book; and if anyone takes away from the words of the book of this prophecy, God will take away his part from the tree of life and from the holy city, which are written in this book. (Revelation 22:18-19)

CONCLUSION

So, "Does God have more to say?" No, God does not have more to say because He has said everything He wanted to say in the written Word. We "hear God's voice" when we read and study the Living Word (Hebrews 4:12) and when the Holy Spirit, who breathed it out in the first place, illumines its meaning to our hearts and minds. When faithful preachers, teachers, and witnesses speak from the Word, they are forth-telling from the completed revelation. There is no "new" revelation to be told or received apart from that.

Going back to the Blackabys' thought on the pattern in which God spoke to people, we know that, contrary to what they state, the Bible does not say that God spoke *directly* to all of His people. God only spoke to *particular and chosen* people. The message He gave was intended for all His people, but He didn't just randomly speak to anyone about anything. There was always a clear reason and defined audience. The Bible reveals a consistent pattern of God's people recognizing His revealed truth, first in verbal form and now in written form—as His speech and nothing more!

Remember that just because God spoke in the past—a final and decisive act—does not mean He has finished sovereignly acting in the present. He is always acting and, at times, this is according to His unspoken will. We may not know what He is doing until after the fact, but we must simply rest in Him and trust that His ways are best. He will provide us with comfort and assurance as we simply believe and obey His Word. It is not for us to "hear" more.

3

EXPERIENCING GOD

We must stress that the basis for our faith is neither experience nor emotion, but the truth as God has given it: in verbalized, propositional form in the Scripture and which we first of all apprehend with our minds - though, of course, the whole man must act upon it.[1]

—Francis Schaeffer

The Christian faith is based on the propositional truth found only in God's Word as the great theologian Francis Schaeffer said. We can know God and have a corresponding sense of closeness to Him when He enables our minds to apprehend that truth. This brings us to our second main question: "By what means does God 'come' to us?" In other words, can we know God in ways other than by His Spirit through His Word?

Many today believe that we, through our own chosen means, can know God. They think experiencing God, in our own decided way, is just as important, if not more so, than understanding the truth of Scripture. For example, author Sarah Young, in her popular contemporary book *Jesus Calling,* states, "I knew that God communicated with me through the Bible, but I yearned for more…"[2] What is this "more" that she is longing for? She desires a personal encounter or direct experience with the Living God beyond the Word. Is this something we should desire?

The belief known as mysticism would answer yes. Mysticism says that direct knowledge of God, spiritual truth, or ultimate reality can be attained through subjective experience as intuition or insight.[3] Is that how God gives knowledge of Himself—through our subjective insight? Popular mystic teaching in our day says that we can know God experientially through things such as disciplines, creation, corporate worship, and visions and dreams.

According to Merriam Webster's Dictionary, *experience* means: something personally encountered, undergone, or lived through; direct participation in events.[4] Should we seek to personally encounter God in order to know Him? Should we, like Young, yearn for more than the Bible?

THROUGH DISCIPLINES

Does God come to us through man-invented disciplines? Mystic spirituality greatly influenced the evangelical church through Richard Foster's book *Celebration of Discipline: The Path to Spiritual Growth* first published in 1978 and the edition quoted herein. The book outlines twelve essential disciplines that "move us beyond surface living into the depths" and "invite us to explore the inner caverns of the spiritual realm."[5] According to Foster, these disciplines are so powerful that even a non-believer can employ them. He states:

Recent converts-for that matter people who have not yet turned their lives over to Jesus Christ - should practice them.[6]

If non-believers can attain some spirituality through practicing a discipline, and not by the blood of Christ, we must wonder if this belief system embraces sound doctrine or promotes mystic spirituality. Below are a few quotes to help us determine:

> The imagination is stronger than conceptual thought and stronger than the will. (p 22)
> The inner world of meditation is most easily entered through the door of the imagination. (p 22)
> In learning to meditate, one good place to begin is with our dreams...If we are convinced that dreams can be a key to unlocking the door to the inner world, we can do three practical things...(p 23)[7]

Can human imagination and dreams contribute to successful meditation? Foster goes on to convey that meditation is a particular learned behavior of thinking and centering on one's own thoughts (centering down), in stillness (quietness), and then concentrating to hear God as "the inward living Christ." Within this new centered down position, a person can allegedly invoke Christ's presence. Foster states:

> There is a progression in the spiritual life...This time is for learning to "center down," or what the contemplatives of the middle ages called "re-collection." It is a time to become still, to enter into the recreating silence, to allow the fragmentation of our minds to become centered. (p. 24)
> Another meditation aimed at centering oneself begins by concentrating on breathing...become silent outwardly and inwardly. Be attentive to the inward living Christ...then listen once again. (p. 25)[8]

Foster asserts that if we generate an encounter by what he

defines as meditation on Scripture, Christ will come to us:

> As you enter the story, not as a passive observer but as an active participant, remember that since Jesus lives in the Eternal Now and is not bound by time, this event in the past is a living present-tense experience for Him. Hence, you can *actually* encounter the living Christ in the event, be addressed by His voice and be touched by His healing power. It can be more than an exercise of the imagination; it can be a genuine confrontation. Jesus Christ will actually come to you.[9]

Supposedly, not only will meditation bring Christ to us, it will also take us into God's presence. Foster continues:

> That is why meditation is so threatening to us. It boldly calls us to enter into the living presence of God for ourselves. It tells us that God is speaking in the continuous present and wants to address us.[10]

> One of the fatal mistakes of Israel was their insistence upon having a human king rather than resting in the theocratic rule of God over them...The history of religion is the story of an almost desperate scramble to have a king, a mediator, a priest, a go-between.[11]

It is important to remember that it was God who required the people of Israel to have a mediator, a priest, a go-between. They didn't insist upon it, like they did a king, as Foster implies. Nor was it their prerogative to supply one for themselves. Only God could provide a mediator for them. And He did so in Moses and ultimately in Christ.

Anytime God communicated with His people, there had to be a go-between. Before Christ, God's mediator was Moses. Even Moses could not be in God's presence on his own terms. In Exodus 33, when God speaks to Moses face to face, it is because God initiates and makes provision for communication. Moses is to simply listen to God and then believe and obey

Him in leading the Israelites. However, in typical Moses fashion, he wants proof that God will follow through and be with them. God assures Moses that He will, but then Moses oversteps his boundaries. He says to God, "…show me your glory" (vs. 18). God responds:

> But He said, "You cannot see My face, for no man can see Me and live!" (Exodus 33:20)

Moses was not allowed to go beyond God's self-disclosure, nor could he see God's face directly and live. God did graciously provide a cleft in the rock so that Moses would be protected when God passed by.

God used Moses to go between Him and His people. The Israelites received God's message secondhand, and they were ok with this. In fact, the thought of God speaking directly to them caused great fear and trembling (Exodus 19-20). They did not have an aversion for secondhand messages from God though it seems Foster does:

> Human beings seem to have a perpetual tendency to have somebody else talk to God for them. We are content to have the message secondhand.[12]

Now we see Foster's view that meditation is a learned technique based in human ability. It is employed for the purpose of having a spiritual experience and a corresponding sense of well-being and psychological comfort. Real Christian meditation is not waving some magic wand to bring God into our presence or to hear some inward living voice, nor is it entering into God's presence on our terms. Christian meditation is chewing on the truth of God's self-revelation— His Word.

Many may not realize that Foster comes from a Quaker background. Quakerism teaches that man possesses some "inner light" in that he can experience Christ when He comes to us directly for us to see and hear. This is a form of mysticism. This kind of mystic spirituality has been accepted and popularized within evangelical circles largely due to the influence of Foster's book.

Meditation is only one of many disciplines within mysticism. Other teachings on spiritual formation include lectio divina, yoga, walking labyrinths, consulting spiritual directors, mindfulness therapy, sangha (sitting and walking meditation), and contemplative prayer which may include things such as mantras, prayer circles and breath prayers. Contemplative prayer is defined as two-way communication between us and God; we first pray to God and then if we are open and receptive He will speak to us. This is extremely dangerous because it baits people toward a spiritual reality that is *apart from* God's Word.

Some within evangelicalism currently promote and teach contemplative prayer. For example, American evangelist, author, and Bible teacher Beth Moore[13] says on the *Be Still DVD* that we, like Moses, can hear from God directly, if we are still before Him:

> "The Lord would speak to Moses face to face, as a man speaks with his friend." Exodus 33:10 That's part of contemplative prayer. When we sit back and realize that it is not just that we have something to say to God, it's that God has something He wants to say to us…I want to be in that tent of meeting. I want to be in that place where the cloudy pillar of God's glory falls. And I want to sit back and listen long enough that perhaps the God of all creation might just speak to me.[14]

She says this in light of Psalm 46:10, "Be still and know that I am God" (the DVD's theme verse). She uses this verse along with God's tent of meeting with Moses to say that we should enter the silence so God will speak to us. But God does not speak to us *in the same way* that He did to Moses in the tent of meeting. "Be still" does not mean enter the silence, nor does "know that I am God" mean you must hear God's voice directly.

The correct translation of "be still" in Psalm 46:10 means "cease striving." It means we should stop doing vain activity and rest upon God and His Word. The correct interpretation of the next part "know that I am God" is a demand to recognize that God is God and you are not. God providentially directs and guides us in our circumstances without our consent or knowledge. A good example of this is found in Proverbs 21:1 which says, "The king's heart is like channels of water in the hand of the Lord; He turns it wherever He wishes." We should simply rest on the Lord and realize that He helps people consider certain things by providentially directing them, not verbally speaking to them.

Unfortunately, Moore is teaching contemplative prayer when she uses Psalm 46:10 to mean "be still and enter the silence." Gary Gilley, pastor of Southern View Chapel in Springfield, Illinois, says that spiritual formation shrugs off the principles of the Reformation while making plenty of room for Catholic spirituality:

> Spiritual formation seeks to lure evangelicals into ancient Catholic and Orthodox contemplative practices in order to *draw closer to God, experience His presence, and hear His voice apart from Scripture.* In order to embrace this mystical form of spirituality, contemplatives are willing to compromise at virtually every turn...*Methods never found in the Bible* as the true means of spiritual growth and of knowing God, are emphasized...The contemplatives have sold out to Catholic mysticism and abandoned the clear teaching of Scripture. Sadly, in the process many undiscerning evangelicals will follow suit.[15] (Emphasis added)

A truly advanced spiritual life results from God's work through God's means. It does not result from any of man's fabricated disciplines or techniques.

THROUGH CREATION

Does God come to us through the creation or daily activity? Is it possible to see God through *things*? One popular author, Ann Voskamp of *One Thousand Gifts,* asks, "Do I have eyes to see His face in all things..."[16] When she says this, what is she really asking? Does she desire to possess a particular gaze in order for God to be revealed to her, to commune with God, and to behold a saving God?

God is omnipresent which means that He is everywhere present. He is also transcendent which means that He is altogether different than His creation. The creation only gives us awareness that God exists and has certain qualities. This is called general revelation and there is no need to "obtain" it because we possess it naturally. General revelation does not excuse men from God's wrath:

> For the wrath of God is revealed from heaven against all ungodliness and unrighteousness of men who suppress the truth in unrighteousness, because that which is known about God is evident within them; for God made it evident to them. For since the creation of the world His invisible attributes, His eternal power and divine nature, have been clearly seen, being understood through what has been made, so that they are without excuse. For even though they knew God, they did not honor Him as God or give thanks, but they became futile in their speculations, and their foolish heart was darkened. (Romans 1:18-21)

On the other hand, special revelation is God's truth as revealed in Scripture. It is how He reveals Himself specifically. Not everyone possesses this knowledge, only those who have received the truth.

Voskamp, in asking if she has "eyes to see His face in all things," is essentially seeking for special revelation of God in the creation—where it isn't given. Read the quote in context:

> All beauty is only reflection. And whether I am conscious of it or not, any created thing of which I am amazed, it is the glimpse of His face to which I bow down. Do I have eyes to see it's Him and not the thing?...A pantheist's god is a passive god, but omnipresent God is Beauty who demands worship, passion, and the sacrifice of a life, for He owns it. Do I have eyes to see His face in all things...Faith is in the gaze of a soul. Faith is the seeing soul's eyes upon a saving God, the saving God of twisted bodies, the saving God of harvest moons.[17]

Contemporary author and theologian Bob DeWaay states the error of Voskamp's thinking in his article *Romantic Panentheism, a Review of One Thousand Gifts by Ann Voskamp*:

> That God is not limited spatially (there is nowhere where He is not – Psalm 139:7-10) is a valid, Biblical concept. But panentheism describes an ontological, not spatial category. Ontology is the study of being. It is the study of what something is in its essential nature. Panentheism teaches that God's essence or being is in everything. This is not the doctrine of omnipresence (though it would affirm it). *If God in His essence and essential being is found in everything, then there is nothing unique about Christ* (which is precisely the New Age claim). Biblically, nature does not reveal God and His glory in the same way Christ does. Nature reveals God obliquely and only in a condemning, not saving, way. Christ reveals God in His divine nature and speaks God's inerrant words. Jesus spoke inerrant, binding words that will be our judge on the last day (John 12:48). The moon does no such thing.[18] (Emphasis Added)

God makes Himself truly known, not in one thousand gifts, but in one gift—Christ. He is the living bread come down from heaven. It is only through Him that one can have life:

I am the living bread that came down out of heaven; if anyone eats of this bread, he will live forever; and the bread also which I will give for the life of the world is My flesh. (John 6:51)

He who has the Son has the life; he who does not have the Son of God does not have the life (1 John 5:12)

Again, is that the same thing as what Voskamp states?

The moon has all my gaze, God-glory heavy and mounting. I kneel here, needing to know how a hung rock radiates – ethereal? This beauty is not natural, not of nature...Someone is behind it, in it. Beauty Himself completes. I am alive![19]

Voskamp says that she is alive after gazing at the moon. We know that He is good and blesses all His creatures by the things He has created, but they do not make us "alive." And not even when we see the creation as beautiful and good is it God's means for communion or personal closeness with us:

God is present in all the moments, but I do not deify the wind in the pines, the snow falling on hemlocks the moon over harvested wheat. Pantheism, seeing the natural world as divine, is a very different thing than seeing divine God present in all things...[20]

We are hungry. We eat. We are filled...and emptied. And still, we look at the fruit and see only the material means to fill our emptiness. We don't see the material world for what it is meant to be: *as the means to communion with God.*[21]

God's means of communion with us is through the truths of God's Word, not the material world. God reveals Himself generally through the creation. The creation is not God's means to see a saving God or give us life. It is only through Christ that God saves. Then, communion with God comes by His Spirit through the Word. Not through created things.

Voskamp has a few accurate statements and good quotes,

yet they are intertwined with quotes from Catholics who teach and promote mysticism. For instance, she quotes favorably from Luther, Augustine, Irenaeus, Elisabeth Elliot, John Calvin, and John Owen. And she also quotes favorably from Catholics such as Erasmus, Brennan Manning, St. Francis de Sales, Julian of Norwich, Teresa of Avila, and Henri Nouwen.[22] But the lingo of mysticism is not the same as the truth of Scripture, and so completely opposite views should not be quoted together as though they are analogous. Bob DeWaay says it very concisely and pointedly:

> Mysticism and the practices Voskamp endorses that promote it, do lead to a Cosmic Christ, that is a creation-centered one rather than the Christ who bodily ascended to heaven and is seated at the right hand of God. The mystical Christ is immanent only, not transcendent. He is contacted by unbiblical, mystical means rather than through the gospel that saves us from God's wrath against sin.[23]

Christians should shun the idea of embracing both mystic thought and accurate theological thought. Instead, we should battle against mysticism's deceptive influences. This is what the Reformers, such as Martin Luther, did. They actively opposed Catholic mysticism. David Wells, a professor at Gordon-Conwell Theological Seminary, describes what took place:

> What was revolutionary about the Protestant Reformers was their insistence that God is not savingly known through created nature as paganism had proposed, or through human nature as the medieval mystics had thought (and some evangelicals now think), or through the Church and its sacraments as the Roman Catholic Church taught, but directly, by the work of the Holy Spirit and the truth of the biblical Word, the internal and supernatural work of the Spirit creating the spiritual climate in which Scripture might be received. The Reformers rejected all assertions that there are channels of saving grace in nature,

human nature, or the Church. They held that there are no intermediaries between God and the sinner save for Christ himself, and they insisted that this unique role could not be usurped without destroying the faith that claimed his name.[24]

THROUGH CORPORATE WORSHIP

Does God come to us through man's creations during corporate worship? Can we truly know and worship God when we visually enhance and artistically enrich our corporate worship gatherings? What do we mean? Well, as an example, an evangelical university magazine states they want their students to see and hear God during chapels:

> Whatever an individual's preference or learning style, we want people to say, *'Wow, I really saw God.'*...recent chapels featured a student artist creating paintings during several messages, original skits by the theatre department, and sacred dance. This diverse palette of creativity allows attendees to experience the Lord, in new ways. Some people "hear" God speak through the message, and others through dance, worship, or images.[25] (Emphasis added)

But, as we saw in the last chapter, God only makes Himself personally known through His Word. God did not choose to reveal Himself through images, dance, theatre, and art. No matter how great we make them, they do not enable us to know Him, though many worship leaders would want us to believe so. The Second Commandment helps us understand this. Here is Charles Spurgeon's take on it:

> There are still many who worship idols and images, but they say, 'No, we do not worship them; we worship God through them.' Just so, but that is as much forbidden in the Second

Commandment as the worship of other gods is forbidden in the First--they are both violations of the Divine Law![26]

Why, then, would we attribute authority to things God never intended us to use for knowledge and worship of Him? Some may ask, like in the Heidelberg Catechism:

> Question 98. But may not images be tolerated in the churches, as "books to the laity"?
> Answer: No: for we must not pretend to be wiser than God, who will have his people taught, not by dumb images, but by the lively preaching of his word.[27]

True worship of God happens only as a result of the preaching and teaching of God's Word and embracing its truth. It is then that the Holy Spirit, by His power and presence, enables us to worship God in His way—in spirit and in truth:

> But an hour is coming, and now is, when the true worshipers will worship the Father in spirit and truth; for such people the Father seeks to be His worshipers. God is spirit, and those who worship Him must worship in spirit and truth. (John 4:23-24)

Just because someone uses their God-given artistic talent to create something beautiful or pleasant does not make the object revelatory. Thus, it should not be used or viewed as such. Again, God's Word is the only means for that. Unfortunately, the university magazine article is describing a worship that is sensual in nature and that is not rooted in a Scriptural foundation of worship.

Quite possibly, no one has elevated a sensual understanding of worship more than Bill Johnson, pastor of Bethel Church in Redding, California, and author of *When Heaven Invades Earth Expanded Edition*. In chapter four "Faith-Anchored in the Unseen", he conveys some faulty thinking about worship by linking it to an unscriptural understanding of faith:

Many of us have thought that the ability to see into the spiritual realm is more the result of a special gift than an unused potential of everyone…Herein lies the secret to the supernatural realm that we want restored to the Church. Jesus told us that He only did what He *saw* His Father do. Such an insight is vital for those who want more. The power of His actions-for instance, the mud in the eye of the blind-is rooted in His ability to see…God is very committed to teaching us how to see…Learning how to see is not the purpose for our worship, but it is a wonderful by-product.[28]

Do humans have the ability to see into the spiritual realm? Was Jesus anointed with some spiritual seeing ability? Johnson says Jesus had a seeing ability into the spiritual realm as a man and that He used it to learn things by watching His Father. Was Jesus seeing into the spiritual realm when He said He only does what He sees His Father doing?

The "spiritual realm" that Johnson speaks of is what he believes to be the things concerning God and His Kingdom. That realm is only known to us through God's Word. Not in our ability to see through a mystical, sensual experience. In John 5:19, when Jesus said that He only does what He sees His Father doing it was to affirm His divinity. Read it in context:

For this reason therefore the Jews were seeking all the more to kill Him, because He not only was breaking the Sabbath, but also was calling God His own Father, making Himself equal with God. Therefore Jesus answered and was saying to them, "Truly, truly, I say to you, the Son can do nothing of Himself, unless *it is* something He sees the Father doing; for whatever the Father does, these things the Son also does in like manner. (John 5:18-19)

Jesus, being the divine Son, always acts in complete unity with His Father, and He always knows what His Father is doing.

Further, according to Johnson, if you jump into the mystical and sensual worship that has been provided, there will also be benefits for both individuals and the church as a whole:

> Not only is all ministry to be Spirit empowered, it is to have a *gathering element* to it…The anointing equips us to bring the world into an encounter with God. That encounter is what we owe them.[29]

It is as though the church is indebted to the world and can, with an anointing, bring the world into the presence of God, i.e. have an encounter with God. Though a popular notion, the power and presence of God cannot be invoked by man nor is it something the church owes the world. Johnson's "seeing faith" is not based in spirit and in truth, and so it cannot be the by-product of real worship. Seeing God is actually rooted in utilizing the mind to read His Word, and then understanding, believing and obeying it from the heart. We can only see what God has revealed. God does not give us some spiritual "sense" other than that.

Artistically enhanced services do not lend a hand or add to God's *only* way of revealing Himself—through His Word. True worship, whether it be in song, in prayer, in silence, in our work, in our testimony, etc., happens as a response to God's Word whether hearing it read or preached, or God bringing its truth to our remembrance. But in providing a *sensual atmosphere*, many worship leaders and modern worship settings emphasize something God never intended.

THROUGH VISIONS AND DREAMS

Does God come to us through visions and dreams? Scripture records people having visions and dreams such as Peter's dream of a sheet coming down out of heaven in Acts 10, or Paul's vision of a man of Macedonia calling to him in Acts 16. Paul's vision was for God to redirect him to preach the gospel in Macedonia. Peter's dream was God revealing the power of the gospel to cleanse all—Gentiles as well as Jews. Any vision or dream recorded in Scripture occurred for the purpose of God revealing truth or giving authoritative direction. But do visions and dreams that occur today happen for that same revelatory reason?

The desire to tell about visions and dreams is quite popular today. A perusal of a typical Christian bookstore makes this very apparent:

— *Heaven is For Real* by Todd Burpo
— *90 Minutes in Heaven* by Don Piper
— *Proof of Heaven* by Eben Alexander
— *To Heaven and Back* by Mary C. Neal, M.D.
— *My Journey to Heaven* by Marvin Bestemen with Lorilee Craker

But why are they popular? Do they entail new revelation of some kind? Ezekiel says:

> Her prophets have smeared whitewash for them, seeing false visions and divining lies for them, saying, 'Thus says the Lord God,' when the Lord has not spoken. (Ezekiel 22:28)

People can have visions that are not revelation from the Lord. Thus, we should consider the validity and source of any supposed vision or dream as if from God. If it did actually occur, it does not mean it was from God.

There was a time when the people of God were asked to receive messages from the realm of the dead. In response, Isaiah wrote, "To the law and to the testimony! If they do not speak according to this word, it is because there is no light in them" (Isaiah 8:20 NKJV). Just because someone claims to have received a fresh word, does not mean that they actually received it from God.

What if the vision or dream does have a portion of truth in

it? What if it includes some content that lines up with Scripture? Does that validate it as a direct revelatory act of God speaking? No, the two are not equal because only Scripture is God's completed revelatory Word. If God supernaturally acts such as performing a miracle, it does not mean God is speaking or revealing something through it. God's wonders stand on their own as does the truth of Scripture. We may "see" or "experience" His marvelous wonders, but we dare not attribute any authoritative speech in conjunction with His mighty works. They simply are what they are. So yes, it is possible to have a seemingly good vision or dream and it not come from God. Martin Lloyd-Jones explains the dynamic of having supposed revelatory experiences very well when he says:

> Let us imagine I follow the mystic way. I begin to have experiences; I think God is speaking to me; how do I know it is God who is speaking to me? How can I know I am not speaking to man; how can I be sure that I am not the victim of hallucinations, since this has happened to many of the mystics? If I believe in mysticism as such without the Bible, how do I know I am not being deluded by Satan as an angel of light in order to keep me from the true and living God? I have no standard.... *The evangelical doctrine tells me not to look into myself but to look into the Word of God; not to examine myself, but to look at the revelation that has been given to me.* It tells me that God can only be known in His own way, the way which has been revealed in the Scriptures themselves.[30] (Emphasis Added)

So what exactly is the source of such experiences? It is possible that Satan could be the one behind some experience. Rev. Dr. R. Fowler White says:

> The issue in this discussion, therefore, cannot be, "Have (or haven't) you experienced the Spirit's supernatural, revelatory work?" Rather the issue is, "What have you experienced? A work of the Holy Spirit or a work of some other agency (human or demonic).[31]

The bottom line is that we should never think experiences can trump God's completed Word. The apostle Peter, in his experience known as the Transfiguration, actually saw Jesus Christ's glory and heard the majestic voice, and yet did he promote and tell everyone about his experience? No, Peter reports it as Scripture and then directs our attention not to his experience, but to something else:

> For we did not follow cleverly devised tales when we made known to you the power and coming of our Lord Jesus Christ, but we were eyewitnesses of His majesty. For when He received honor and glory from God the Father, such an utterance as this was made to Him by the Majestic Glory, "This is My beloved Son with whom I am well-pleased"—and we ourselves heard this utterance made from heaven when we were with Him on the holy mountain. *So* we have the prophetic word *made* more sure, to which you do well to pay attention as to a lamp shining in a dark place, until the day dawns and the morning star arises in your hearts. But know this first of all, that no prophecy of Scripture is *a matter* of one's own interpretation, for no prophecy was ever made by an act of human will, but men moved by the Holy Spirit spoke from God. (2 Peter 1:16-21)

Peter does not say, "You, too, should hear and can have…so seek for it." Instead, he says that he was there, heard, and saw, so pay attention to what is written! Huge difference!

SUMMARY

Mysticism can and has influenced evangelicalism. Many, in churches, pursue experiences over truth. For instance, they seek to "find their burning bush," "have fresh encounters with Jesus," "hear the living voice," and "go deeper with God." Such quests do not root a person in the sole authority of Scripture but instead take them beyond it.

The actual biblical experience we need is to believe and obey God. *That* experience comes when our minds are renewed by the truth of Scripture (Romans 12:1-2). Benjamin Warfield, former professor at Princeton Theological Seminary, explained the difference between biblically experiencing God and mystical experience:

> Evangelical Christianity interprets all religious experience by the normative revelation of God recorded for us in the Holy Scriptures and guides, directs, and corrects it from these Scriptures, and thus molds it into harmony with what God in His revealed Word lays down as the normal Christian life. The mystic, on the other hand, tends to substitute his religious experience for the objective revelation of God recorded in the written Word. The result is that the external revelation is relatively depressed in value, if not totally set aside.
>
> In the history of Christian thought *mysticism* appears accordingly as that tendency among professing Christians which *looks within*, that is, to the religious feelings, in its search for God. It supposes itself to contemplate within the soul the movements of the divine Spirit, and finds in them either the sole sources of trustworthy knowledge of God, or the most immediate and convincing sources of that knowledge, or, at least, a coordinate source of it alongside of the written Word. The characteristics of *Christian mysticism*, from the point of view of religious knowledge, is therefore *its appeal to the "inner light," or "the internal word,"* either to the *exclusion of the external or written Word, or as superior to it* and normative for its interpretation, or at least as coordinate authority with it, this "inner light" or "internal word" being conceived not as the rational understanding but as the immediate deliverance of the religious sentiment."[32] (Emphasis added)

Again, "By what means does God 'come' to us?" God does not come through experiences or encounters. God *came* personally in the God-Man, Jesus Christ, and died once for all. He was raised and ascended to the right hand of the Father.

And we now know Him by His Spirit through His Word. This is how He personally displays His glory to the believer and how His Spirit testifies to the truth of Christ. God "now comes" by His means which is His revealed Word. We are close with Him as we hear, believe, and obey that Word. Feeling close to God can only happen when His Spirit bears witness, concerning these things, to our spirit.

4

TELLING "YOUR" STORY

*Because errors and heresies were likely to creep into
the church, by which the minds of many professing
Christians would be corrupted...People must hear,
and ministers must preach, for the time to come, and
guard against the mischiefs that are likely to arise
hereafter, though they do not yet arise. They will turn
away their ears from the truth; they will grow weary
of the old plain gospel of Christ, and then they will be
greedy of fables, and take pleasure in them, and God
will give them up to those strong delusions, because
they received not the truth in the love of it...*[1]

—Matthew Henry

The gospel is first and foremost about God Himself. It is
about His holiness, power, love, and glory. It is about Him
saving a people for Himself. It is clear and has some definitive
points including the fall of man, God's attributes, the nature of
salvation, the person of Christ, the consequences of sin, as well
as the conclusion of this present evil age. These points are vital
to the integrity of the whole message. If any point is omitted or
placed in a different context, it can alter the overall gospel
story and inaccurately portray God.

Matthew Henry, the great English Presbyterian minister, as

stated above, pointed out that people will grow weary of God's story. They will turn away from truth in want of fables. Is this happening in our day? Are the plethora of "Christian" movies, books, skits, dramas, sermons, and songs representative of such a time? Are they accurately depicting God's story, or, by being altered, are they proof that people are not interested in the "old plain gospel of Christ?" This chapter tackles the third main question: "Can God's story be your story?" We need to clarify both the real biblical story and its central figure. In doing this, we will be able to identify if our current culture is interested in God's story or their own stories.

MYTHOLOGIZED

In 2 Timothy 4:1-4, Paul writes:

> I solemnly charge *you* in the presence of God and of Christ Jesus, who is to judge the living and the dead, and by His appearing and His kingdom: preach the word; be ready in season *and* out of season; reprove, rebuke, exhort, with great patience and instruction. For the time will come when they will not endure sound doctrine; but *wanting* to have their ears tickled, they will accumulate for themselves teachers in accordance to their own desires, and will turn away their ears from the truth and will turn aside to myths. But you be sober in all things, endure hardship, do the work of an evangelist, fulfill your ministry. (2 Timothy 4:1-4)

We see here that myths are what people will turn to when they do not want to hear truth. They turn to myths to soothe their own desires instead of the conviction that comes from sound doctrine.

Perhaps surprisingly, the people who want to hear myths are those within a ministry context. Paul tells Timothy to respond by avoiding and opposing myths and by continuing to preach the Word with clarity. Matthew Henry further explained this passage in 2 Timothy:

> Observe, (1.) These teachers were of their own heaping up, and not of God's sending; but they chose them, to gratify their lusts, and to please their itching ears. (2.) People do so when they will not endure sound doctrine, that preaching which is searching, plain, and to the purpose; then they will have teachers of their own. (3.) There is a wide difference between the word of God and the word of such teachers; the one is sound doctrine, the word of truth, the other is only fables. (4.) Those that are turned unto fables first turn away their ears from the truth, for they cannot hear and mind both, any more than they can serve two masters. Nay, further, it is said, They shall be turned unto fables. God justly suffers those to turn to fables who grow weary of the truth, and gives them up to be led aside from the truth by fables.[2]

The Greek word for "myth" is *muthos* and its meaning is rather complex. Myths generally refer to made-up stories such as those from ancient Roman and Greek culture. Those stories define how things were or came to be in that particular culture. Myths can also be defined as any false idea or fictitious viewpoint. Myths, as we talk about them in this chapter, have to do with false ideas regarding actual events. They ultimately create a different story than the original.

In talking about myths, we must not be confused with allegory. A faithful allegory of truth is completely different than a myth which changes the message of truth from within. There have been some faithful allegories regarding the gospel or the Christian walk written in church history such as *Pilgrim's Progress* by John Bunyan. To be clear, when we talk about myths, we are referring to a contextual reworking of biblical stories that result in an altogether different story.

Myths most often do not outwardly deny truth. They actually come in the form of truth, but undercut the truth by way of substitution. This leads the mind astray with thoughts that are not right. Paul was afraid of this with the Corinthians:

> But I am afraid that, as the serpent deceived Eve by his
> craftiness, your minds will be led astray from the simplicity and
> purity *of devotion* to Christ. 2 Corinthians 11:3

Referring to this text, J.C. Ryle stated:

> Since Satan cannot destroy the gospel, he has too often
> neutralized its usefulness by addition, subtraction, or
> substitution...Now this "cunningness," Paul tells us, is precisely
> what we have to fear in false doctrine. We are not to expect it to
> approach our minds in the garment of error, but in the form of
> truth.[3]

We must always pay attention because myths could be in our very midst. To help, let's look at a few of today's popular stories to see if they are portraying truth in its fullness or some form of myth.

"Simplified for Children" - Truth or Myth?

A popular kids' Bible book, *The Jesus Storybook Bible,* by Sally Lloyd-Jones opens with:

> God wrote, 'I love you'– he wrote it in the sky, and on the earth,
> and under the sea. He wrote his message everywhere! Because
> God created everything in his world to reflect him like a mirror –
> to show us what he is like, to help us know him, to help our
> hearts sing...and God put it into words, too, and wrote it in a
> book called 'the Bible.'"[4]

As we stated in chapter 2, the creation is not God's means to reveal Himself or commune with us in a personal or saving way. The fact that Lloyd-Jones says God wrote His message everywhere should immediately make us cautious of what else might be in the book. Let's continue. In the third chapter titled "The Terrible Lie," we read:

"Does God really love you?" The serpent whispered [to Eve]...Eve picked the fruit and ate some. And Adam ate some, too. And a terrible lie came into the world. It would never leave. It would live on in every human heart, whispering to every one of God's children: "God doesn't love me?"[5]

Was that really the terrible lie—that "God doesn't love me?" No, the actual terrible lie was when Satan told Eve that if she ate the fruit she would not really die but would be like God knowing good and evil. Satan seduced her by claiming that the knowledge of good and evil was something good that God was withholding from her.

After Eve and Adam ate, what came into the world was God's just judgment of death upon their sin. The storybook continues:

Later that evening, as God was taking his walk, he called to them, "Children?"[6]

Was that really what God called Adam and Eve after having sinned? No, they were not His children at that point. On the contrary, they were separated from God by their rebellion, and God carried out His just judgment against them by bringing the curses. Is this what Lloyd-Jones describes? She states the following:

And though they would forget him, and run from him, deep in their hearts, God's children would miss him always, and long for him - lost children yearning for their home.[7]

She says Adam and Eve were lost and yearned for their home. Was that really the case? No, they ran from God because they were ashamed of their sin and knew they were in trouble.

So God came looking for that which was lost. He could have sent the judgment of death immediately, but in His grace, He withheld. The account unfolds as seen in Genesis 2 & 3:

The Lord God commanded the man, saying, "From any tree of the garden you may eat freely; but from the tree of the knowledge of good and evil you shall not eat, for in the day that you eat from it you will surely die." (Genesis 2:16-17)

Indeed, has God said, "You shall not eat from any tree of the garden?...You surely will not die! For God knows that in the day you eat from it your eyes will be opened, and you will be like God, knowing good and evil." (Genesis 3:1b-5)

Then the Lord God called to the man, and said to him, "Where are you?" He said, "I heard the sound of You in the garden, and I was afraid because I was naked; so I hid myself." (Genesis 3:9-10)

And Paul, in referring to the event, says:

Therefore, just as through one man sin entered into the world, and death through sin, and so death spread to all men, because all sinned. (Romans 5:12)

So, does it seem that the remainder of Lloyd-Jones' storybook is going to retell the biblical story just in cute kids' terms? To tell, read the invitation at the end of the storybook:

For anyone who says yes to Jesus
For anyone who believes what Jesus said
For anyone who will just reach out to take it
Then God will give them this wonderful gift:
To be born into
A whole new Life...[8]

Pause there. This sounds reasonable, right? We should take God's free gift and believe and receive Jesus to have new life, right? But we must keep reading:

...To be who they really are
Who God always made them to be –

42

Their own true selves –
God's dear
Child.
Because, you see, the most wonderful thing about this Story is –
it's your story, too![8]

Is this God's salvation described in Scripture? Does God rescue people, through some enlightenment or reshaping, back to their true selves? Or, does God rescue sinful people from death and darkness by recreating them in Christ and giving them life and light? Scripture gives us a clear answer:

> Therefore if anyone is in Christ, *he is* a new creature; the old things passed away; behold, new things have come. (2 Corinthians 5:17)

> For He rescued us from the domain of darkness, and transferred us to the kingdom of His beloved Son, in whom we have redemption, the forgiveness of sins. (Colossians 1:13-14)

So the main concern with this storybook is not that it doesn't have *some* facts in it. The main concern is that it couches biblical characters, events, and terms within a newly defined framework. This alters the story from its biblical context, redefining its message. Would your child be able to discern this story's message from the real one?

"God's Love" - Truth or Myth?
Regarding the nature of God and the punishment of people, well-known author, Rob Bell, in his book *Love Wins*, says the following:

> Of all the billions of people who have ever lived, will only a select number 'make it to a better place' and every single other person suffer in torment and punishment forever? Is this acceptable to God? Has God created millions of people over tens of thousands of years who are going to spend eternity in anguish?

Can God do this, or even allow this, and still claim to be a loving God? Does God punish people for thousands of years with infinite, eternal torment for things they did in their few finite years of life?[9]

Hell is our refusal to trust God's retelling of our story.[10]

Is that what hell is? Hell is the inevitable consequence of man rejecting God. The truth is that because of God's holiness and justice He pronounced the punishment of death upon man's sin. This is not Him being unfair or cruel. Rather, God, in His great love, sent His One and Only Son to shed His blood and provide an escape by becoming a curse for us:

Christ redeemed us from the curse of the Law, having become a curse for us—for it is written, "CURSED IS EVERYONE WHO HANGS ON A TREE." (Galatians 3:13)

It seems Bell is not speaking about the love of the God of the Bible. Instead, it seems, he has skirted around the grace of our wonderful Savior with a "grace" of his own making. In fact, Bell degrades Jesus as some energy force found in everything for sinners to easily access:

[Jesus is] an energy in the world, a spark, an electricity that everything is plugged into.[11]

Paul finds Jesus there, in that rock, because Paul finds Jesus everywhere.[12]

True salvation is sinners being reconciled to God through the blood of Christ, not deity and humanity coming to some connection.

"Anointed Like Jesus" - Truth or Myth?

Bill Johnson says, in his book *When Heaven Invades Earth Expanded Edition,* that in order for Jesus to be a man, He had to put His divinity aside:

> While He is 100 percent God, He chose to live with the same limitations that man would face once he was redeemed...Jesus became the model for all who would embrace the invitation to invade the impossible in His name. He performed miracles, wonders, and signs as a man in right relationship to God...not as God. If He performed miracles because He was God, then they would be unattainable for us. But if He did them as a man, I am responsible to pursue His lifestyle...[13]

> Jesus lived His earthly life with human limitations. He laid His divinity aside (see Phil. 2:5-7) as He sought to fulfill the assignment given to Him by the Father: to live life as a man without sin...[14]

> The anointing is what linked Jesus, the man, to the divine, enabling Him...[15]

> It was the Holy Spirit that revealed the Father to Jesus.[16]

It is incredibly important to remember that while Jesus had two distinct natures—God and man—He only ever functioned as one person—The God-Man. At the incarnation, Jesus did not lay His divinity aside. He performed miracles because of His divine nature—not because He received some divine anointing as a mere man or was linked to divinity.

Johnson seems to teach that Jesus received an anointing to function divinely so he can also teach that the church can receive the same kind of anointing. Philippians 2 is really about Jesus humbling Himself by laying aside His *privileges* as God and clothing Himself with humanity. The Creed of Chalcedon, A.D. 451, clarifies any confusion about the person of Christ:

> ...one and the same Christ, Son, Lord, Only-begotten, recognized in two natures, without confusion, without change, without division, without separation; the distinction of natures being in

no way annulled by the union, but rather the characteristics of each nature being preserved and coming together to form one person and subsistence, not as parted or separated into two persons, but one and the same Son and Only-begotten God the Word, Lord Jesus Christ...[17]

The myth Johnson seems to have created states that the church, with Christ's anointing, can and should invade earth the same way Christ did. The New Testament commission of the church is to *spread the gospel*, not to usher in God's presence (heaven invading earth) before men. The church can never do what only God in Christ could do. Heaven already "invaded" earth at the incarnation and will only "invade" earth again when Christ returns in visible glory.

"God and Us" - Truth or Myth?

Roma Downey, co-producer of the movie *Son of God* and the television miniseries *The Bible*, and co-author of the book *A Story of God and All of Us.*[18] said what she believes about God's existence in an interview with *The Washington Post*:

> I see God in everyone and in everything. I guess, when I'm looking for inspiration myself I probably find it most in nature and the beauty and magnificence of nature...There are two points of view perhaps: That there is no God, or there is only God. And for me there is only God. Um, it's like you can see nothing as a miracle or you can see everything as a miracle, right?[19]

Most people, if you asked them, would probably say they thought Downey's re-makes were in fact telling the biblical account. Nevertheless, based on her statements, we must wonder if they are theologically accurate. This should give us better insight as to what *A Story of God and All of Us* is actually about. Because Downey believes everyone and everything is God, it would only follow that her understanding of salvation is some enlightenment. But this is impossible because of the transcendent nature of God —distinct, above, and separate from His creation:

> Yours, O Lord, is the greatness and the power and the glory and
> the victory and the majesty, indeed everything that is in the
> heavens and the earth; Yours is the dominion, O Lord, and You
> exalt Yourself as head over all. (1 Chronicles 29:11)

Could *A Story of God and All of Us* actually be about a "merging" of characters rather than one recreating the other?

....

As we just saw, with only a few of countless examples, myths, whether presented by the world or the visible church, can generate a sundry of theological problems. Yet it appears there is already an audience for myths. *The Huffington Post* reported in December of 2013 that *The Jesus Storybook Bible* reached 1 million copies sold.[20] Rob Bell, in 2011, made *Time* magazine's list of the "100 Most Influential People in the World."[21] First published in 2003, *When Heaven Invades Earth* has since published a daily devotional and journal (2005), a revised edition (2009), an expanded edition (2013), and a teen guide version (2014).[22] Lastly, an article in the April 2013 edition of *The Hollywood Reporter* stated, "Mark Burnett and Roma Downey's *The Bible* is shattering sales records in its first week of home video release, selling 525,000 units to become the top-selling TV miniseries of all time."[23]

As we saw from 2 Timothy 4, people are attracted to myths because they would rather have their ears tickled. Myths do not deliver truth in its full conviction. They instead cater to people's natural sinful desires. They weave in a pleasant story that ultimately replaces the real story. This craving is well-explained by John MacArthur in *The MacArthur Bible Commentary*:

They have an itch to be entertained by teachings that will produce pleasant sensations and leave them with good feelings about themselves.[24]

The "good" feelings myths can give have nothing to do with the power of the gospel and the delight found only in Christ. It is only the power of God's gospel that can truly satisfy a person. And it satisfies by giving completely new thoughts and desires. Charles Spurgeon stated:

> But what was this gospel which achieved so much? Was it a thing palatable to human nature? Did it offer a paradise of present happiness? Did it offer delight to the flesh and to the senses? Did it give charming prospects of wealth? Did it give licentious ideas to men? No; it was a gospel of morality most strict, it was a gospel with delights entirely spiritual—...And yet it spread. Why? My friends, I think the only answer I can give you is, because it has in it the power of God.[25]

VAIN PHILOSOPHIES & EMPTY DECEPTION

Some biblical remakes may seem relatively innocent, yet if they alter the message in any way, they dishonor God and are an affront to His person. In the case that alterations are made, sound teaching ends up being replaced by vain philosophies and empty deceptions. Matthew Henry explained the difference when he said:

> There is a philosophy which is a noble exercise of our reasonable faculties, and highly serviceable to religion, such a study of the works of God as leads us to the knowledge of God and confirms our faith in him. But there is a philosophy which is vain and deceitful, which is prejudicial to religion, and sets up the wisdom of man in competition with the wisdom of God, and while it pleases men's fancies ruins their faith.[26]

Vain philosophies and empty deceptions ultimately rob people of the joy and salvation found only in Christ. Paul explains this in 2 Corinthians:

> *We are* destroying speculations and every lofty thing raised up against the knowledge of God, and *we are* taking every thought captive to the obedience of Christ, and we are ready to punish all disobedience, whenever your obedience is complete. (2 Corinthians 10:5-6) (Emphasis added)

Regarding the term "speculations," *The MacArthur Study Bible* states, "Thoughts, ideas, reasoning, philosophies, and false religions are the ideological forts in which men barricade themselves against God and the gospel."[27] But God's wisdom in Christ is what we need according to Paul:

> For indeed Jews ask for signs and Greeks search for wisdom; but we preach Christ crucified, to Jews a stumbling block and to Gentiles foolishness, but to those who are the called, both Jews and Greeks, Christ the power of God and the wisdom of God. Because the foolishness of God is wiser than men, and the weakness of God is stronger than men. (1 Corinthians 1:22-25)

One example of man's wisdom, foundational to the whole church-growth movement, can be found in Robert Schuller's book *Self Esteem: The New Reformation.* He states:

> Label it a 'negative self-image,' but do not say that the central core of the human soul is wickedness. If this were so, then truly, the human being is totally depraved. But positive Christianity does not hold to human depravity, but to human inability. I am humanly unable to correct my negative self-image until I encounter a life-changing experience with non-judgmental love bestowed upon me by a Person whom I admire so much that to be unconditionally accepted by him is to be born again.[28]

Schuller suggests that a negative self-image is man's root

flaw which places us in a state of inability and fear, not depravity, and that to be born again is being delivered into a positive Christianity.

However, the real good news is not the wearing of rose-colored glasses. The real good news is first bad news—we are sinful and hopelessly lost. The good news is that a Deliverer was sent! Has Schuller, as quoted, described the Deliverer and new birth? This is in fact the wisdom of man, not God. This can be most destructive in a church setting:

> But false prophets also arose among the people, just as there will also be false teachers among you, who will secretly introduce destructive heresies, even denying the Master who bought them, bringing swift destruction upon themselves. Many will follow their sensuality, and because of them the way of the truth will be maligned; and in *their* greed they will exploit you with false words; their judgment from long ago is not idle, and their destruction is not asleep. (2 Peter 2:1-3)

In the Greek text, "secretly introduce" is translated from a word meaning "to bring in, in addition."[29] The action is camouflaged and stealth-like. Teachers, who are among the people, appear true but actually bring in false teachings—as if it were the truth.

We cannot assume safety from such teachers just because we are in a church setting. When empty deception crept into the Colossian church, Paul taught them truth and exhorted them to guard their minds. They were to identify the particular false teaching and not accept it. Paul instructs:

> See to it that no one takes you captive through philosophy and empty deception, according to the tradition of men, according to the elementary principles of the world, rather than according to Christ. For in Him all the fullness of Deity dwells in bodily form, and in Him you have been made complete. (Colossians 2:8-10a)

HIS STORY, YOUR TESTIMONY

The gospel is good news in that God sent His Son to the earth to become the substitutionary atonement for man's sin. Man, although created in God's image, rebelled against God, thus becoming the object of His wrath. Christ, the only perfect sacrifice, died, was buried and rose again to save a people for God His Father. Christ died for man but unto God. He did this as a substitute and bore the curse which we deserved. That is how much God loved us!

One noteworthy item regarding this gospel story is that it is God's story from start to finish. It greatly affects man, but it occurred outside of man. Michael Horton, author of *In the Face of God*, writes:

> Biblical Christianity is concerned with what happened outside us, 2,000 years ago, outside the city of Jerusalem. It is an "over there" religion, not an "in here" religion. It is centered on what happened externally, not on what happens internally.[30]

The gospel is *for* man in that it personally saves him, and it is God's regenerating power that changes a human heart. The announcing of the gospel is the means whereby a person believes and receives its truth:

> So faith *comes* by hearing, and hearing by the word of Christ. (Romans 10:17)

Repentance and faith is what happens as the result. Horton further explains:

> Christianity does not announce to the world, "If you have a conversion experience, you will be saved, so make sure you have a conversion experience." Anything that has to do with me and my works or my experience securing victory and intimacy with

God is sure to lead to despair. It is bad news, not good. And, by the way, this is not to in any way detract from the importance of the new birth or the subjective dimension of Christian experience. It is simply to say that nothing that happens within me is the gospel.[31]

So, a Christian's story, also known as a personal testimony, should be testament to the truthfulness of God's saving story. When someone talks about "their faith," it should be about the power and the effect of the gospel story in their life. If you listen closely, many of the personal stories told today do not actually reflect that reality.

The Old Testament emphasizes that God wants absolutely no rivals—because there are none! God's story, the revelation of Himself in the person and work of Christ, is what should capture our hearts. If that story is twisted to highlight man instead of God, it has lost its focus. Worse than that, it is idolatry.

Let's now correctly answer, "What is the biblical story and who is its central figure?" The biblical story is God doing a work and saving a people for His glory and their good! It is based in the finished work of Jesus Christ. The story should not be subtly repainted or rewoven. It should never rob God of His wisdom in Christ. It dare not be altered or refocused because He is only truly given the glory when we stick with His story!

5

A FRAMEWORK OF SELF

The unhealthy state of the church at this time is due in large part to a low view of God. This, in turn, has led to a high view of man. Not until there is the restoration of an elevated view of God will the church be restored to her former glory and have an effect upon the world again.[1]

—Steve Lawson

The human heart naturally has a low and unbiblical view of God. It invariably follows that it has a high view of itself instead as Lawson mentioned. Whether people consciously think about it or not, their natural predetermined mindset is interest in themselves. But apart from God, man is self-deceiving and wicked. Scripture paints the true picture of man:

> The heart is more deceitful than all else And is desperately sick; Who can understand it? (Jeremiah 17:9)

> For even though they knew God, they did not honor Him as God
> or give thanks, but they became futile in their speculations, and
> their foolish heart was darkened. (Romans 1:21)

Even when we give attention to deity, without the light of God's Word, it is self-regarding. In fact, it is quite possible to think we have turned our eyes toward God when in reality we have kept them upon ourselves. R.C. Sproul, in Ligonier Ministries' May 2014 newsletter, indicates that a man-centered theology has invaded the Christian culture. He pointedly asks:

> Is the center, the driving force of your theology, God or man?
>
> Of course, the answer should be God. Yet I can't tell you how often I've heard well-meaning preachers talk about the gospel without mentioning God's glory and His gracious sovereignty in salvation. We're swimming against the tide to remain God-centered, as the pull to ignore God's glory has been strong since our first parents fell in the garden.
>
> Man-centered theology leads to emotional manipulation wherein thousands are coerced into making false professions of faith. It minimizes our radical corruption as sinners and God's power to save His people for His glory.
>
> ...a God-centered theology [is one] that is faithful to all of Scripture, one that has been passed down through history by the greatest preachers and teachers of the Christian faith...[2]

There currently exist churches that operate out of a man-centered framework though they would not give that impression outwardly. Think about the following statements:

> — Our worship is real, authentic, and powerful.
> — We are a community that will connect you to God and others.
> — Embark on your spiritual journey here and begin your adventure with Jesus.

These slogans could easily be heard from many local churches. But, does simply advertising the presence of authentic worship equate to an actual biblical understanding of authentic worship? And, does connecting with a community mean having a biblical understanding of true fellowship and walking in the Light as He is in the Light (1 John 1:7)? Finally, does having an adventure with Jesus include the reality of suffering for the gospel?

In other words, could many be pretending homage to God yet with hearts submitted to their own advantage? The great theologian, Stephen Charnock, stated it well:

> No duty can be spiritual that hath a carnal aim; where God is the sole object, he ought to be the principal end; in all our actions he is to be our end, as he is the principle of our being;...Self is the spirit of carnality; to pretend a homage to God and intend only the advantage of self, is rather to mock him than worship him. When we believe that we ought to be satisfied, rather than God glorified, we set God below ourselves, imagine that he should submit his own honor to our advantage; we make ourselves more glorious than God, as though we were not made for him, but he hath a being only for us; this is to have a very low esteem of the majesty of God. Whatsoever any man aims at in worship above the glory of God that he forms as an idol to himself instead of God, and sets up a golden image, God counts not this as worship.[3]

CHURCH-GROWTH PRAGMATICS

The fascination with self may have had more influence in the church than we realize. In fact, it may have been the reason why church-growth pragmatics gained a foothold.

The theory of church-growth pragmatism was expressed and implemented into evangelicalism predominantly by Robert Schuller. It was birthed at Fuller Seminary through the teachings of Donald McGavran and C. Peter Wagner. Bob DeWaay, in his book *Redefining Christianity,* gives us more insight into Schuller and his working:

> Robert Schuller invented it when he began his ministry in California in the 1950's. Schuller's idea was to make a church that un-churched people would find appealing…Schuller developed and perfected this non-offensive message and eventually turned it into the Crystal Cathedral and the "Hour of Power." His Institute for Successful Church Leadership has trained many of the key leaders that are currently promoting the seeker model within evangelicalism, including Bill Hybels and Rick Warren.[4]

The seeker model pushes truth aside for a tangible concern. It is predominantly concerned with producing results such as having a large attendance. It doesn't matter how a crowd is drawn together as long as it is. Gary Gilley, in his book *This Little Church Went to Market,* describes this:

> Growing churches are creating an atmosphere, an environment of fun. So fun has replaced holiness as the church's goal. Having a good time has become the criterion of an excellent, growing church, since fun and entertainment is what consumers want. Yet Scripture references encouraging churches to become havens of fun are, as one may suspect, sadly lacking.[5]

A pragmatic mentality in the church is similar to a consumer mentality in the marketplace. In the supply and demand theory, the supply is always affected by the demand, and the demand always determines the supply. The church takes on a supplier role and varies their supply based on the individual church goer who is usually happy to take on the role of consumer. The individual's preferences—demand—set the criteria for the church's message and function—supply. In order to reach the world and get them into church, the church must give them what they "demand" such as fun.

56

But the local church should not gather *for* non-believers', that is, with their interests in mind. John MacArthur, in his book *Reckless Faith*, states the error in the consumer approach:

> Many Christians have the misconception that to win the world to Christ we must first win the world's favor. If we can get the world to like us, they will embrace our Savior. That is the philosophy behind the user-friendly church movement...The express design of this user-friendly philosophy is to make unconverted sinners feel comfortable with the Christian message. People won't come to hear the Gospel proclaimed. Give them something they want. Put on a show. Entertain them. Avoid sensitive subjects like sin and damnation. Accommodate their worldly desires and felt needs. Slip in the Gospel in small, diluted doses. The whole point is to make the church a place where non-Christians can enjoy themselves. The strategy is to tantalize non-Christians rather than confront their unbelief. That is altogether incompatible with sound doctrine. It is compromise with the world. James called it spiritual adultery (James 4:4).[6]

Is providing an enjoyable atmosphere what it means to "reach the unreached?" No, Christians "reach" unbelievers by telling them what they *need* to hear as fallen creatures—the gospel. The church that tells people what they *want* to hear is one of compromise. Oswald Chambers, in his book *The Psychology of Redemption*, powerfully explained what happens when the church succumbs to compromise:

> Will the church that bows down and compromises succeed? Of course it will; it is the very thing that the natural man wants. This line of temptation as revealed by our Lord is the most appallingly subtle of all...The temptation to win and woo men is the most subtle of all, and it is a line that commends itself to us naturally. But you cannot win and woo a mutiny; it is absolutely impossible. You cannot win and woo the man who, when he recognizes the rule of God, detests it...The only way in which the Kingdom of God can be established is by the love of God as

revealed in the Cross of Jesus Christ, not by the loving-kindness of a backboneless being without justice or righteousness or truth. The background of God's love is holiness. His is not a compromising love, and the Kingdom of our Lord can only be brought in by means of His love at work in regeneration.[7]

Charles Spurgeon summed up the vanity of church-growth pragmatism quite well more than a century ago:

> If we add to our Churches by becoming worldly, by taking in persons who have never been born again; if we add to our Churches by accommodating the life of the Christian to the life of the worldling, our increase is worth nothing at all; it is a loss rather than a gain! If we add to our Churches by excitement, by making appeals to the passions rather than by explaining the truth of God to the understanding; if we add to our churches otherwise than by the power of the Spirit of God making men new creatures in Christ Jesus, the increase is of no worth whatever.[8]

The church's first priority should be preaching Christ crucified and calling people to repentance. This is the only true way to add numbers to God's church as stated in Acts:

> Peter *said* to them, "Repent, and each of you be baptized in the name of Jesus Christ for the forgiveness of your sins; and you will receive the gift of the Holy Spirit." (Acts 2:38)
> So then, those who had received his word were baptized; and that day there were added about three thousand souls. (Acts 2:41)
> And the Lord was adding to their number day by day those who were being saved. (Acts 2:47b)

God adds to His church by making people new creatures in Christ. We cannot add to the church on our own terms. Church-growth occurs by sowing the Word of God, not getting more people in the doors. Astoundingly, church-growth pragmatism has overcome what were once doctrinally sound churches. It has happened slowly, methodically, and, has been fully integrated in many local churches without much awareness.

PARADIGM SHIFT

How has church-growth pragmatics overcome so many churches? The Word of God is the standard and framework for Christian operation. A shift from God's Word results, not merely in a variation of methods, but in a completely different message.

The word "paradigm" is variously defined by Merriam-Webster as: pattern, example, philosophical or theoretical framework of any kind, archetype.[9] It can be generalized as the "set standard or framework" of any subject area from which one is to operate. A paradigm *shift* is when the set standard is changed.

A paradigm shift could be a good thing depending on the subject matter. For example, when it was discovered that the world was not flat and revolved around the sun, people's thinking about the solar system changed, and for the better. In that case, a paradigm shift was good!

A paradigm shift within Christendom is deadly. And it doesn't happen overnight. It happens over time as truths are ignored or redefined. It might look something like this:

— Truths are ignored when some truths are "left out" of preaching such as the sinfulness of man, the cost of discipleship, hatred by the world, and the sufferings associated with believing. These "hard" truths are overlooked essentially developing a whole new criteria.

— Some truths have a different meaning when other truths are dismissed. It puts them in a different light and gives them new meaning. For example, when the concepts of sin and God's holy wrath are absent, the love of God can imply a personal, sentimental kind of love. This conveys God as a romantic rather than a holy and loving redeemer.

— When truths are ignored or redefined, they are ultimately replaced with error. People not steeped in actual truth, easily become susceptible to error. Error is then entrenched as if it were truth.

This very thing has occurred in the church over the past 40 to 50 years. It has permitted duplicity of thought to enter in through its passivity to compromise. We saw this in the previous chapters where skewed theology is passing as sound doctrine. The result is a paradigm shift away from the sole authority of Scripture. And the younger generation knows nothing different. Unfortunately, it seems they are simply along for the ride.

6

DISGUISED REDIRECTION

If what has turned you away from your object has been a bad thought, a bad doctrine, bad teaching, a bad motive—that never came from God, that must be from Satan.[1]

—Charles Spurgeon

S atan would like no more than for Christians to believe lies. So he comes to us secretly, cleverly, and with a purpose. He works behind the scenes in hopes to effectively usurp God's authority. It is of utmost importance that we grasp the fact that Satan's work is most often not visible or obvious. The following text in Isaiah reveals the nature of Satan:

> How you have fallen from heaven, O star of the morning, son of the dawn! You have been cut down to the earth, You who have weakened the nations! But you said in your heart, "I will ascend to heaven; I will raise my throne above the stars of God, and I

will sit on the mount of assembly in the recesses of the north. I will ascend above the heights of the clouds; I will make myself like the Most High." (Isaiah 14:12-14)

This passage, as understood by many scholars over the centuries, is two-fold in meaning. First, Isaiah prophesies that the King of Babylon will exalt his kingdom above God. Secondly, Isaiah discloses that there is a power behind the King of Babylon—Satan. John MacArthur gives further explanation in *The MacArthur Study Bible*:

> Jesus' use of v. 12 to describe Satan's fall (Lk 10:18; cf. Rev12:8—10) has led many to see more than a reference to the king of Babylon. Just as the Lord addressed Satan in His words to the serpent (Gen 3:14, 15), this inspired dirge speaks to the king of Babylon and to the devil who energized him. See Ezek. 28:12-17 for similar language to the king of Tyre and Satan behind him.[2]

Satan works behind the scene and in disguise. Dr. Steven Riser, author of *Deception: Discerning the Devil's Most Dangerous Device* writes:

> If I tempted you, you would know it. If I deceived you, you wouldn't know it. If you know you are being deceived, then you are not being deceived. Eve was deceived because she believed the lie that God did not want what was best for her, but didn't know it was a lie. We can see from Genesis 3 that deception was the primary strategy of Satan from the beginning. Perhaps some of us look down on Eve for being deceived by the serpent in the garden? But each time we sin we're deceived by the same lie.[3]

The elusive character of Satan fooled even the Jewish leaders. They were being led astray and they did not know it was the devil leading them. Jesus had to point it out to them. Even then, because of their sinful hearts, they did not believe nor like what Jesus said:

Why do you not understand what I am saying? *It is* because you cannot hear My word. You are of *your* father the devil, and you want to do the desires of your father. He was a murderer from the beginning, and does not stand in the truth because there is no truth in him. Whenever he speaks a lie, he speaks from his own *nature*, for he is a liar and the father of lies. (John 8:43-44)

Nonetheless, we can recognize the results of Satan's activities because, whether overt or subtle, they do not line up with God's truth.

BIG-TENT CHRISTIANITY

As we saw in the last chapter, evangelicalism in general has shifted away from the Word of God. This has allowed for the influence of various movements such as:

— Church-Growth Movement: emphasizes the church's duty to be sensitive to seekers & connect with unbelievers

— Charismatic Movement: moves people into an experienced-based faith

— Word-Faith Movement: attempts a role reversal and attributes to man authority that only God possesses

— Signs & Wonders Movement: provides "powerful works" for people to believe in a powerful presence

— Emergent Church Movement: approves the idea of discussing doctrine, but not coming to clarity

— The New Apostolic Reformation: goes beyond the Charismatic Movement to the absolute authority of modern day apostles and prophets

— Spiritual Formation/Contemplative Movement: seeks encountering Christ by man's efforts through techniques, disciplines, or "spiritual" experiences

Evangelicalism has been converging with these false movements creating a whole new entity. Some have referred to it as Big-Tent Christianity.

Big-Tent Christianity claims to be a massive move of the Spirit. It asserts that the Spirit is directly, mystically, and sensually revealing His presence *in the church* and speaking fresh words *to and through the church.* The problem: this supposedly happens apart from the Word. The Spirit's "voice" is only heard *in the Scripture* when He illumines its truth to us. Sinclair Ferguson, former Professor of Systematic Theology at Westminster Theological Seminary, in contrasting the Reformation with Medieval theology, explains:

> The canon for Christian living has increasingly been sought in a 'Spirit-inspired' living voice within the church rather than in the Spirit's voice heard in Scripture. What was once little more than a mystical tendency has become a flood. But what has this to do with the medieval church? Just this. The entire medieval church operated on the same principle, even if they expressed it in a different form: the Spirit speaks outside of Scripture; the believer cannot know the detailed guidance of God if he tries to depend on his or her Bible alone.
>
> Not only so, but once the 'living voice' of the Spirit has been introduced it follows by a kind of psychological inevitability that it is this living voice which becomes the canon for Christian living.
>
> This view--inscripturated Word plus living voice equals divine revelation--lay at the heart of the medieval church's groping in the dark for the power of the gospel. Now, at the end of the second millennium we are on the verge--and perhaps more than the verge of being overwhelmed by a parallel phenomenon. The result then was a famine of hearing and understanding the Word of God, all under the guise of what the Spirit was still saying to the church. What of today?[4]

The desire in seeking "to hear the Spirit's voice in the church" in actuality becomes a drift from the anchor of truth.

Doctrinal truth—referred to as walls—are then torn down. Biblically sound doctrine is trivialized and compromised. The mixture is evident when:

— The Word of God is taught in conjunction with an appeal to self-fulfillment.
— Worship times are more of a production than a response to God and His Word.
— Being a Christian is minimized to "Following Christ" instead of "Following Christ and suffering for His namesake."
— Church events are more for connecting and socializing than walking in the Light.
— Embracing people trumps embracing a firm stance on the Word.
— Evangelizing, conferencing, and networking become a mingling with teachers and people with questionable beliefs.
— Being missional is now the power of God unto salvation.
— Devotion to God alone is now having a passion for _____ (fill in the blank).

Though Big-Tent Christianity promotes going to church, having fellowship, having passion, and doing missions, it lacks the centrality of the gospel and tenacity for truth. It is an entity redirected away from a Christian foundation.

A GOSPEL OF PURPOSE

A major turn in direction occurred when a different gospel entered the church, with little commotion and much hype. At the turn of the century, Rick Warren's campaign 40 Days of

Purpose® was launched. Warren had previously established his presence in the church at large with his book *The Purpose Driven Church* published in 1996. The campaign included the book *The Purpose Driven Life* along with a video *40 Days of Purpose: Small Group & Sunday School Video Curriculum.* In the first session of the video, Warren gives a supposed gospel presentation and salvation invitation.[5] But he does not mention Jesus going to Calvary to die for our sins, being buried, and raised from the dead. In actuality, Warren exalted man's purpose in life and used God's name to do it. Yet he has viewers, those who would like to receive Jesus into their lives, follow him in a prayer and welcomes those who prayed that prayer into the family of God.

How can someone be assured of their salvation when they have not heard and received the actual gospel? Yet many trusted leaders allowed Warren's "gospel" to enter their church. For the most part, it was well-received by people. Many did not see its flaws and jumped on board. Some had questions about it, but were unable to pinpoint the exact error. And still others felt completely rebuffed. Bob DeWaay writes:

> The reason people are feeling disenfranchised from their congregations is that when a church becomes Purpose Driven, it changes the very core of its identity. The change from existing to feed Jesus' flock to existing to feed the appetites of religious consumers is drastic and systemic.[6]

Because of Warren's campaign, the majority of people in churches now have an altered purpose. Their new basis of existence is due to what has been termed "the new gospel." Gary Gilley explains it well:

> The new gospel is a liberation from low self-esteem, a freedom from emptiness and loneliness, a means of fulfillment and excitement, a way to receive our heart's desires, a means of meeting our needs. The old gospel is about God; the new gospel

is about us. The old gospel is about sin; the new gospel is about our needs. The old gospel is about our need for righteousness; the new gospel is about our need for fulfillment. The old gospel is foolishness to those who are perishing; the new gospel is attractive. Many are flocking to the new gospel but it is altogether questionable how many are actually being saved.[7]

The Westminster Catechism states that the chief end of man is to "glorify God and to enjoy Him forever."[8] The new gospel has man's satisfaction as its hidden undercurrent. It is no longer that man has a chief end of glorifying God. It is that God has a chief end of giving man what he wants. A recent article by Harry Reeder in *Tabletalk Magazine* explains this transformation:

> The first question of our new catechism is now, "What is the chief end of God?" The answer: "To love me and make me happy."[9]

It is true that God is concerned with our needs, but His glory is not dependent on our contentment. This happens as He teaches us His ways and we walk in His truth:

> Teach me Your way, O Lord; I will walk in Your truth; Unite my heart to fear Your name. I will give thanks to You, O Lord my God, with all my heart, And will glorify Your name forever. (Psalm 86: 11-12)

Jesus says in John 17 that it is His priority to glorify the Father and He does this by making His name known:

> Jesus spoke these things; and lifting up His eyes to heaven, He said, "Father, the hour has come; glorify Your Son, that the Son may glorify You. (John 17:1)

> Now, Father, glorify Me together with Yourself, with the glory which I had with You before the world was. "I have manifested

Your name to the men whom You gave Me out of the world; they were Yours and You gave them to Me, and they have kept Your word." (John 17:5-6)

Do the majority have this kind of priority? Or, is it possible, that Warren's campaign led to many churches becoming full of people focused on their own false purpose as if it were to God and His glory? Was God's name exalted or man's?

CONCLUSION

The true gospel is the power of God unto salvation. It must be proclaimed in its fullness to be effective. A different gospel, one of purpose, cannot do what only God's gospel can do. Yet Satan despises the true gospel and the new birth provided in Christ Jesus. He does whatever it takes to bring whoever he can to a false consensus. With things where they currently stand, it seems many are on board with the redirection. John MacArthur, in his book *The Truth War,* states:

> Where are the men and women today with the courage to stand alone? The church in our age has abandoned a confronting stance. Instead of overturning worldly wisdom with revealed truth, many Christians today are obsessed with finding areas of agreement. The goal has become integration rather than confrontation. As the church absorbs the values of secular culture, it is losing its ability to differentiate between good and evil. What will happen to the church if everyone proceeds down the slippery path of public opinion?[10]

The people of God need to acknowledge Big-Tent Christianity and then defend the true faith from that which is only Christian by name. After all, could God be allowing Big-Tent Christianity to occur to bring His final judgment?

7

FALLING AWAY FORETOLD

*And the apostle Paul mentioneth… "There must,"
saith he, "be a falling away," or an apostasy from the
faith, under the leading of "the man of sin."*[1]

—John Owen

In light of Big-Tent Christianity and its ever increasing presence, we should search Scripture to know what part it plays in God's overarching plan as this present evil age unfolds. Scripture tells of a final falling away from the faith that will occur in the church at the end of the age. This brings us to an eschatological discussion. There are a wide range of viewpoints regarding the last things, and many already have their minds made up regarding the subject. It does not hurt to consider again what Scripture has to say. In this chapter, we will zero in on passages found in 2 Thessalonians and

Revelation to gain perspective. This may challenge us and push the envelope of our thinking a bit, but please read in light of considering God's Word.

THE DAY OF THE LORD

At one point, the Thessalonian church believed the day of the Lord was at hand. This was because they had given ear to false teaching. Paul addresses their confusion and tells them not to listen to anyone who says the day of the Lord has come for the very reason that two particular events must occur first:

> Now we request you, brethren, with regard to the coming of our Lord Jesus Christ and our gathering together to Him, that you not be quickly shaken from your composure or be disturbed either by a spirit or a message or a letter as if from us, to the effect that the day of the Lord has come. Let no one in any way deceive you, for *it will not come* unless the apostasy comes first, and the man of lawlessness is revealed, the son of destruction. (2 Thessalonians 2:1-3)

Paul points them to the fact that two certain events—the apostasy and the revealing of the man of lawlessness—will occur before the day of the Lord. These hadn't happened, so he directs them to not be disturbed as if that day was immediately upon them. Paul reiterates they should not be taken captive by rumors because there will be clear signs that the day of the Lord is at hand!

There are a couple of noteworthy items found in this passage. Notice the chronology of events is clear: apostasy, man of lawlessness revealed, day of the Lord. And, notice it is the *brethren* (saints) who will see these two things happen *first* (before The Day of the Lord). It is why they are not to be disturbed. Also, in all of chapter two, Paul uses the definite article "the" 13 times. *A series of definite articles this long in the Bible is rather unique!* What does it mean? It means there is only *one* apostasy like *this* apostasy, and there is only *one* man of lawlessness like *this* man of lawlessness, etc.

APOSTASY IN THE VISIBLE CHURCH

The word "apostasy," when used in the Bible, comes from a few different Greek words. They are variously translated as "falling away," "rebellion," "abandonment." Normally, though, "apostasy" is applied with the understanding of falling away from a supposedly held religious position. The following two texts are examples of a Greek form of the word "apostasy" translated "fall away:"

> Take care, brethren, that there not be in any one of you an evil, unbelieving heart that falls away from the living God. (Hebrews 3:12)

> But the Spirit explicitly says that in later times some will fall away from the faith, paying attention to deceitful spirits and doctrines of demons. (1 Timothy 4:1)

The meaning of the word "apostasy" as it appears in 2 Thessalonians 2 is determined from its context. It is a religious falling away. Those who claimed to be Christian, but really were not, will noticeably reject the doctrines of the true faith. Those who were not true converts will give ear to antichrists that come from within to deceive them. People who do not have true faith will be led away from truth:

> Children, it is the last hour; and just as you heard that antichrist is coming, even now many antichrists have appeared; from this we know that it is the last hour. They went out from us, but they

were not *really* of us; for if they had been of us, they would have remained with us; but *they went out*, so that it would be shown that they all are not of us. (1 John 2:18-19)

John Calvin pointed out how apostasy occurs:

…For when apostasy is made mention of without anything being added, *it cannot be restricted to a few.* Now, none can be termed apostates, but such as have previously made a profession of Christ and the gospel. Paul, therefore, predicts *a certain general revolt of the visible Church.*[2] (Emphasis added)

Charles Spurgeon concurred when he stated:

There are many such spirits that are constantly rising up, not outside the Church—there, we could deal with them—but *inside* the Church, using the Words of Truth, and the signs of Truth to signify something far other than the Truth of God![3]

Many apostasies have occurred within the church, but this context also shows that the apostasy mentioned here is referring to the final one before the Lord's return. It will be of a critical nature because it is associated with the final antichrist.

It should be noted that the apostasy and the revealing of the man of lawlessness, the Antichrist, are interrelated. Although this person is spoken of a number of times in Scripture, this is the only context that says he will be revealed. So, the two items, the apostasy and his revealing, are concurrent with one another.

ANTICHRIST REVEALED IN TEMPLE

Think back to the garden for a moment. Adam and Eve initially had their eyes on the true and living God as source for knowledge and life. Then Eve was lied to: "The serpent said to the woman 'You surely will not die! For God knows that in the day you eat from it your eyes will be opened, and you will be like God, knowing good and evil'" (Genesis 3:4-5). She was convinced by Satan that it was in her best interest to replace God. When Adam and Even disobeyed, they proved their intent to run their own ship.

The idea of replacing God is seen in the Greek prefix "anti." It means "against" or "in the place of, in the stead of." As previously noted, many who are *anti*-Christ have arisen from within the visible church. Disguised as though they serve and follow Christ, in actuality they attempt to "displace Christ." Similarly, the man of lawlessness is *anti*-Christ in that he attempts to displace the real Lord Jesus Christ:

> Who opposes and exalts himself above every so-called god or object of worship, so that he takes his seat in the temple of God, displaying himself as being God. Do you not remember that while I was still with you, I was telling you these things? And you know what restrains him now, so that in his time he will be revealed. (2 Thessalonians 2:4-5)

It says the man of lawlessness opposes and exalts himself, so that he "takes his seat in the temple of God." What does that mean? Does he actually sit in a literal building? Some think this refers to a rebuilt Jewish Temple in Jerusalem. However, we must consider something. If the Jews were allowed to rebuild their own Jewish Temple, they would probably follow the instructions given in the Old Testament. Do those instructions include a "seat" like this? There was a mercy-seat in the old temple, but that is nothing like this seat. This seat in 2 Thessalonians 2 has the idea of being in the place or position to execute authority. It is not a literal seat in a literal building.

Before the mid nineteenth century, many preachers and scholars understood "the temple" in this text to refer to the visible church and *not* a literal rebuilt Jewish temple. For example, in Charles Spurgeon's sermon titled "Pride the Destroyer" (on Habakkuk 2:4), he references 2 Thessalonians 2 and translates it as the visible church and not a Jewish temple in Jerusalem.[4] Also, in Matthew Henry's commentary regarding 2 Thessalonians 2:4, he states:

> As God was in the temple of old, and worshipped there, and is in and with his church now, so the antichrist mentioned here is some usurper of God's authority in the Christian church, who claims divine honors;...[5]

The church being referred to as the temple of God is also seen in 1 Corinthians 3:16 where Paul uses the same Greek word for "temple" in describing the body of Christ. "The temple of God" in 2 Thessalonians 2:4 is no different. Antichrist will place himself in a position of authority within the visible church. This will occur during the final apostasy of the visible church.

He will portray himself as God by supplanting Christ's authority through his own teachings, leadership, and presence. John Calvin saw it similarly. He stated:

> ...for Paul places Antichrist nowhere else than in the very sanctuary of God. For this is not a foreign, but a domestic enemy, who opposes Christ under the very name of Christ...[6]

Now, some will equate the events of 2 Thessalonians 2 with the abomination of desolation that takes place in Daniel 9 and Matthew 24. However, the details of each event are clearly different, so we should not try to make any parallels other than that they both refer to the same person, Antichrist.

THE MYSTERY OF ANTICHRIST

You would think a man of lawlessness would be recognized right away. But Paul says there is a mystery at work:

> For the mystery of lawlessness is already at work; only he who now restrains *will do so* until he is taken out of the way. (2 Thessalonians 2:7)

Puritan theologian Thomas Manton says of 2 Thessalonians 2:7:

> What is the mystery of iniquity? I answer - The design of usurping Christ's kingdom, and his dignities and prerogatives over the church, to countenance the kingdom of sin and darkness, under the mask of piety and religion. Surely it is something, quite contrary to the gospel, which is the 'mystery of godliness,' 1 Tim. 3:16. So that this mystery is such a course and state design as doth frustrate the true end and purpose of the gospel, and yet carried on under a pretense of advancing and promoting it.[7]

The mystery of the Antichrist is his initial portrayal. He cleverly disguises who he is by a seeming propagation of truth. Antichrist's initial workings within the visible church will be very stealth-like and seem honorable, yet there will be a point when his disguise is unmasked:

> Then that lawless one will be revealed whom the Lord will slay with the breath of His mouth and bring to an end by the appearance of His coming; that is, the one whose coming is in accord with the activity of Satan, with all power and signs and false wonders. (2 Thessalonians 2:8-9)

His evil tactics will be disclosed at some point as John Calvin said:

...and inasmuch as the temple of God itself would be polluted by sacrilegious tyranny, so that Christ's greatest enemy would exercise dominion there. The term revelation is taken here to denote manifest possession of tyranny, as if Paul had said that the day of Christ would not come until this tyrant had openly manifested himself, and had, as it were, designedly overturned the whole order of the Church...[8]

Antichrist's initial "honorable" position of authority will eventually translate into a world-wide rule. It will be tyrannical for those who refuse to submit.

ANTICHRIST'S REIGN

In verses 9-10 of 2 Thessalonians 2, Paul states there is sinister activity with the coming of Antichrist:

That is, the one whose coming is in accord with the activity of Satan, with all power and signs and false wonders, and with all the deception of wickedness for those who perish, because they did not receive the love of the truth so as to be saved. (2 Thessalonians 2:9-10)

We must remember the activity is sinister because it is in accordance with Satan. Revelation 13 records a "wondrous" event of Antichrist—also referred to as the first beast:

I saw one of his heads as if it had been slain, and his fatal wound was healed. And the whole earth was amazed *and followed* after the beast. (Revelation 13:3)

The exact details of this event are not clear. We do know that the beast will receive a fatal wound and then be healed causing the world to be amazed. Some think the symbol of a head slain and wound healed is used metaphorically to describe the revival of a previous world empire. Some think it is actually referring to the person of Antichrist. Either way, the event leads to the world's bedazzlement of Antichrist.

But might this be one of Satan's false wonders? In fact, according to verse 4, Satan—referred to as the dragon—is behind this in order to lead to the worship of Antichrist:

> They worshiped the dragon because he gave his authority to the beast; and they worshiped the beast. (Revelation 13:4a)

There is yet another beast in Revelation 13—the second beast. He is called the false prophet (Revelation 19:20, 20:10) and is given power and authority by Satan to move the peoples of the world toward worship of the image of the first beast. He also performs miraculous signs:

> And he deceives those who dwell on the earth because of the signs which it was given him to perform in the presence of the beast, telling those who dwell on the earth to make an image to the beast who had the wound of the sword and has come to life. And it was given to him to give breath to the image of the beast, so that the image of the beast would even speak and cause as many as do not worship the image of the beast to be killed. (Revelation 13:14-15)

It says the second beast gives breath to the image of the first beast. The English word "breath" is used for the Greek word "spirit." So, the false prophet propagates or enlivens the worship of the image of the first beast. What is this image? Many view it as a literal statue that is somehow placed in a rebuilt Jewish temple. This may or may not be true depending on if you take the "image" as a literal, physical emblem. Either way, do not miss the spiritual significance: people who do not love the truth will gladly worship that which is false.

One way the false prophet moves people toward worship of Antichrist is by motivating and empowering them to come

77

under Antichrist's economic system called the ten horns. We see this in Revelation:

> Then I saw a beast coming up out of the sea, having ten horns and seven heads, and on his horns *were* ten diadems, and on his heads *were* blasphemous names. (Revelation 13:1b)

> And he causes all, the small and the great, and the rich and the poor, and the freemen and the slaves, to be given a mark on their right hand or on their forehead, and *he provides* that no one will be able to buy or to sell, except the one who has the mark, *either* the name of the beast or the number of his name. (Revelation 13:16-17)

Antichrist will have full rule over the earth by this over-arching economic control. He exercises this control when ten authorities give him their allegiance. People of the world will display their own self-interest and worship of the first beast by receiving the mark associated with his authority.

Another of Antichrist's characteristics is realized in Revelation 17 when he is referred to as the Scarlet Beast:

> Then one of the seven angels who had the seven bowls came and spoke with me, saying, "Come here, I will show you the judgment of the great harlot who sits on many waters, with whom the kings of the earth committed *acts of* immorality, and those who dwell on the earth were made drunk with the wine of her immorality." And he carried me away in the Spirit into a wilderness; and I saw a woman sitting on a scarlet beast, full of blasphemous names, having seven heads and ten horns. The woman was clothed in purple and scarlet, and adorned with gold and precious stones and pearls, having in her hand a gold cup full of abominations and of the unclean things of her immorality, and on her forehead a name *was* written, a mystery, "BABYLON THE GREAT, THE MOTHER OF HARLOTS AND OF THE ABOMINATIONS OF THE EARTH." And I saw the woman

drunk with the blood of the saints, and with the blood of the witnesses of Jesus. When I saw her, I wondered greatly. (Revelation 17:1-6)

The Great Harlot represents the entirety of all false religion, which is a self-exalted and false spirituality. Antichrist supports and sustains her, and she gladly sits on Antichrist. He supports and directs the Great Harlot like a pawn for his own purposes. After all, he will already have proven himself quite capable in religious matters, having led an apostasy of the church.

To conclude, the Bible gives only some details regarding the end of this present evil age. We know for sure that there will be a final earthly ruler in Antichrist amidst an apostasy. The authority God gives to Satan and Antichrist will only last for a clearly defined time and has a fixed outcome:

> And he will make a firm covenant with the many for one week, but in the middle of the week he will put a stop to sacrifice and grain offering; and on the wing of abominations *will come* one who makes desolate, even until a complete destruction, one that is decreed, is poured out on the one who makes desolate. (Daniel 9:27)

> And the devil who deceived them was thrown into the lake of fire and brimstone, where the beast and the false prophet are also; and they will be tormented day and night forever and ever. (Revelation 20:10)

Are you currently seeing evidence of a final apostasy? If so, remember God is in control and will help believers while accomplishing His purposes.

8

TWO DISTINCT CITIES

*Enter through the narrow gate; for the gate is wide
and the way is broad that leads to destruction, and
there are many who enter through it. For the gate is
small and the way is narrow that leads to life, and
there are few who find it. (Matthew 7:13-14)*

—Jesus Christ

G od's Word clearly teaches that there are currently two
cities being built. One is a manmade city of destruction
and the other is a heavenly city of everlasting splendor. Each
has their own path and gate.

The two cities are very different with very different
inhabitants. Yet both cities' paths proclaim, "This way to the
glorious city." How do we know which is really the glorious
city? The only way to discern is according to some key "truth-
bearings" found in the Word of God.

The heavenly city that is built by God has a narrow path and
narrow gate. Few find it. Those who do, by faith have obeyed

and received God's saving promise in the gospel. They worship the true and living God:

> By faith Abraham, when he was called, obeyed by going out to a place which he was to receive for an inheritance; and he went out, not knowing where he was going...for he was looking for the city which has foundations, whose architect and builder is God. (Hebrews 11:8-10)

> And I saw the holy city, new Jerusalem, coming down out of heaven from God, made ready as a bride adorned for her husband. (Revelation 21:2)

> And every created thing which is in heaven and on the earth and under the earth and on the sea, and all things in them, I heard saying, "To Him who sits on the throne, and to the Lamb, *be* blessing and honor and glory and dominion forever and ever." (Revelation 5:13)

The other city that is manufactured by man and of *earthly* splendor and majesty has a broad path and wide gate. Those on their way to it are in rebellion to God and worship something other than the true and living God. God will ultimately judge it and bring about its ruin:

> And the kings of the earth, who committed *acts of* immorality and lived sensuously with her, will weep and lament over her when they see the smoke of her burning, standing at a distance because of the fear of her torment, saying, "Woe, woe, the great city, Babylon, the strong city! For in one hour your judgment has come." (Revelation 18:9-10)

> They worshiped the dragon because he gave his authority to the beast; and they worshiped the beast, saying, "Who is like the beast, and who is able to wage war with him?" (Revelation 13:4)
> All who dwell on the earth will worship him, *everyone* whose name has not been written from the foundation of the world in

the book of life of the Lamb who has been slain. (Revelation 13:8)

And it was given to him to give breath to the image of the beast, so that the image of the beast would even speak and cause as many as do not worship the image of the beast to be killed. (Revelation 13:15)

In fact, these verses are evidence that God will allow for a very visible false worship at the end of the age. As we saw in the previous chapter, it is during the last days that an outward worship of Antichrist will occur. It will be those on the broad path who worship Antichrist. True saints will reject worshipping Antichrist just like the saints of Daniel 3 rejected false worship.

All the while, those on the broad way will convince themselves they are not false worshippers but are merely participating in the enjoyments of those headed toward the benevolent city:

There is a way *which seems* right to a man, But its end is the way of death. (Proverbs 14:12)

Some of these false worshippers might even call Jesus Lord, but ultimately do not really know Him:

Many will say to Me on that day, "Lord, Lord, did we not prophesy in Your name, and in Your name cast out demons, and in Your name perform many miracles?" And then I will declare to them, "I never knew you; DEPART FROM ME, YOU WHO PRACTICE LAWLESSNESS." (Matthew 7:22-23)

Those on the broad way are in rebellion to God despite what might seem to be an outward appearance of fidelity. So even when the spiritual landscape appears shiny, it could really be of a majority who think they're heading toward the benevolent city but, in reality, are heading to the manmade city.

The saints of God need to understand the dynamics leading up to and during end-time events. The external and social pressure toward false worship will be great. The delusion will come across as very enticing, even for God's own. They will be pressed toward it but ultimately will not succumb:

> For false Christs and false prophets will arise and will show great signs and wonders, so as to mislead, if possible, even the elect. (Matthew 24:24)

ON BOARD

Those who are truly of the elect will be identifiable for a few certain reasons. They will remain faithful to God and His Word no matter what. Their zeal for truth will compare to the New Testament Bereans who examined Scripture to test even what the Apostle Paul told them. The elect will not put up with falsehoods nor associate with those who do:

> Now these were more noble-minded than those in Thessalonica, for they received the word with great eagerness, examining the Scriptures daily *to see* whether these things were so. (Acts 17:11)

> From Your precepts I get understanding; Therefore I hate every false way. (Psalm 119:104)

> For many deceivers have gone out into the world, those who do not acknowledge Jesus Christ as coming in the flesh. This is the deceiver and the antichrist. Watch yourselves that you do not lose what we have accomplished, but that you may receive a full reward. Anyone who goes too far and does not abide in the teaching of Christ, does not have God; the one who abides in the teaching, he has both the Father and the Son. If anyone comes to you and does not bring this teaching, do not receive him into

your house, and do not give him a greeting; for the one who gives him a greeting participates in his evil deeds. (2 John 1:7-11)

Some will insist there is no such thing as guilt by association in the Christian realm. On the contrary, the Apostle John stated the importance of not rubbing elbows with anyone who teaches false things because it is participating in their evil deeds. A continued presence in false company essentially supports them and the false teaching. This subject was important enough to be explained in the June 2014 issue of Ligonier's *Tabletalk Magazine* titled "Guilt by Association." The reason for this is because there are spirits not from God that are at work behind false teachers:

Beloved, do not believe every spirit, but test the spirits to see whether they are from God, because many false prophets have gone out into the world. By this you know the Spirit of God: every spirit that confesses that Jesus Christ has come in the flesh is from God; and every spirit that does not confess Jesus is not from God; this is the *spirit* of the antichrist, of which you have heard that it is coming, and now it is already in the world. (1 John 4:1-3)

We can recognize when the Spirit of God is at work because Jesus Christ will be continually preached. Martin Luther said:

We preach always Him, the true God and man who died for our sins, and rose again for our justification. This may seem a limited and monotonous subject, likely to be soon exhausted, but we are never at the end of it.[1]

The hearers must say: "We do not believe our pastor; [unless] he tells us of another Master, One named Christ. To Christ he directs us; what Christ's lips say we shall heed. And we shall heed our pastor insofar as he directs us to this true Master and Teacher, the Son of God."[2]

Finally, true saints rest truth upon their shoulders even to the point of suffering for it:

> I am writing these things to you, hoping to come to you before long; but in case I am delayed, *I write* so that you will know how one ought to conduct himself in the household of God, which is the church of the living God, the pillar and support of the truth. (1 Timothy 3:14-15)

> Beloved, while I was making every effort to write you about our common salvation, I felt the necessity to write to you appealing that you contend earnestly for the faith which was once for all handed down to the saints. (Jude 1:3)

> For to you it has been granted for Christ's sake, not only to believe in Him, but also to suffer for His sake. (Philippians 1:29)

> If the world hates you, you know that it has hated Me before *it hated* you. If you were of the world, the world would love its own; but because you are not of the world, but I chose you out of the world, because of this the world hates you. Remember the word that I said to you, "A slave is not greater than his master." If they persecuted Me, they will also persecute you; if they kept My word, they will keep yours also. (John 15:18-20)

All Christians undergo some form of persecution at one point or another. It will inevitably come because of their association with Christ. Scottish churchman and poet Horatius Bonar explained it:

> Small may be our strength in these last days. The tide of error, and sin, and worldliness may be running very strong. It may not be easy to confess Christ, or to hold fast His truth. But His grace is sufficient for us; and woe be to us if we give way to the errors of the age, or conform to its vanities, or seek to please its multitudes, either under the dread of public opinion, or the fear of not being reputed 'men of progress,' or the shrinking from

more direct persecution and hatred! Faithfulness to Christ, and to His truth, is everything, especially in days when iniquity shall abound, and the love of many shall wax cold. Fear not! The reward is glorious; the honour is beyond all earthly honours. The contempt and enmity are but for a day; the dignity and the blessedness are forever and ever. Though men call you narrow-minded for cleaving to old truth,—now obsolete, as they say; for 'worship of a book,' or bibliolatry, as they call it; for the stern refusal to lower our testimony to our glorified Lord and coming King? Let us be content to bear reproach for Him and His word. The glory to be given us at His appearing will more than compensate for all.[3]

Now that's the *real* Christian bus headed toward the *real* city of God! Hope you see the difference.

NOTES

Introduction

1. Charles Spurgeon, *Morning by Morning*, (Bridge-Logos Foundation 1998), 245.

Chapter 1 – Think About It

1. Martin Luther, *Luther at the Imperial Diet of Worms (1521).*

Chapter 2 – Hearing God's Voice

1. Charles Spurgeon, *Our Lord's Prayer for His People's Sanctification*, Sermon #1890, delivered on Lord's Day Morning, March 7, 1866.
2. Henry Blackaby & Richard Blackaby, *Hearing God's Voice*, (Nashville: Broadman & Holman Publishers, 2002), cover jacket.
3. Ibid., 2.
4. Louis Berkhof, *Systematic Theology*, (Grand Rapids: WM. B. Eerdmans Publishing Co. 1939, 1941), 34.
5. Wayne Grudem, *The Gift of Prophecy in the New Testament and Today*, (Westchester: Crossway Books, 1988).
6. John Piper, *Using Our Gifts in Proportion to Our Faith, Part 1*, October 10, 2004, http://www.desiringgod.org/sermons/using-our-gifts-in-proportion-to-our-faith-part-1.
7. John MacArthur, *Prophecy Redefined: A Response to John Piper,* March 12, 2014, http://www.gty.org/blog/B140312/prophecy-redefined.
8. John Calvin, *Calvin: Institutes of the Christian Religion*, Vol. 1, (The Westminster Press, 1960), 69.
9. *The Confession of Faith, The Larger and Shorter Catechisms, Of Public Authority in the Church of Scotland*, Chapter 1 Section VI, 21.
10. Martin Luther, *Luther's Works*, Vol. 36: Word and Sacrament II, ed. Jaroslav Jan Pelikan, Hilton C. Oswald, and Helmut T. Lehmann, (Philadelphia: Fortress Press, 1999), 29.

11. Martin Luther, *D. Martin Luthers Werke*, Vol. 8, 143, as cited in *What Luther Says*, 1482-3.
12. William Gurnall, *The Christian in Complete Armor,* Volume 3, Chapter 24, Section 5.

Chapter 3 – Experiencing God

1. Francis Schaeffer, *The Complete Works*, Vol. 3, Book 3, The New Super-Spirituality, (Crossway), 397.
2. Sarah Young, *Jesus Calling*, (Nashville: Thomas Nelson, 2004), xi.
3. *Merriam Webster's Dictionary*, http://www.merriam-webster.com/dictionary/mysticism.
4. *Merriam Webster's Dictionary*, http://www.merriam-webster.com/dictionary/experience.
5. Richard Foster, *Celebration of Discipline: The Path to Spiritual Growth*, (New York: Harper & Row, 1978), 1.
6. Ibid., 2.
7. Ibid., 22, 23.
8. Ibid., 24, 25.
9. Ibid., 26.
10. Ibid., 19.
11. Ibid., 19.
12. Ibid., 18.
13. From Wikipedia, *Beth Moore*, http://en.wikipedia.org/wiki/Beth_Moore.
14. Beth Moore, *Be Still: and Know That I am God*, DVD, (Fox Faith, 2006).
15. Gary Gilley, *Think on These Things Articles: Contemplative Prayer*, (April/May 2012 - Volume 18, Issue 2), http://www.svchapel.org/resources/articles/22-contemporary-issues/761-contemplative-prayer.
16. Ann Voskamp, *One Thousand Gifts*, (Grand Rapids: Zondervan, 2010), 112.
17. Ibid., 112.
18. Bob DeWaay, *Romantic Panentheism, a Review of One Thousand Gifts by Ann Voskamp*, Issue 120, 2012, http://www.cicministry.org/commentary/issue120.htm.

19. Ann Voskamp, *One Thousand Gifts*, (Grand Rapids: Zondervan, 2010), 109.
20. Ibid., 110.
21. Ibid., 16.
22. Ibid., 233-237.
23. Bob DeWaay, *Romantic Panentheism, a Review of One Thousand Gifts by Ann Voskamp,* Issue 120, 2012, http://www.cicministry.org/commentary/issue120.htm.
24. David F. Wells, *No Place for Truth: Or Whatever Happened to Evangelical Theology?*, 143-144.
25. Suzanne Yonker, *Now Is the Time to Worship*, (Bethel Magazine: Fall 2011), 24. http://www.bethel.edu/news/publications/bethel-magazine/fall-2011.
26. Charles Spurgeon, *Ruins*, Sermon #2565, February 11, 1883, http://www.ccel.org/ccel/spurgeon/sermons44.xvi.html.
27. Heidelberg Catechism, http://www.wts.edu/resources/creeds/heidelberg.html.
28. Bill Johnson, *When Heaven Invades Earth Expanded Edition*, (Destiny Image, Inc., 2013), 46-47.
29. Ibid., 151.
30. Martyn Lloyd-Jones, *Fellowship with God*, (Wheaton: Crossway, 1993), 95.
31. R. Fowler White, *Whatever Happened to the Reformation?*, (Phillipsburg: P&R Publishing, 2001), 165.
32. Benjamin B. Warfield, First published in *The Biblical Review*, (vol. 2, 1917), 169-191; reprinted in *The Works of Benjamin B. Warfield* (Grand Rapids: Baker Book House, 1991, vol. 9), 649-666, http://reformedliterature.com/warfield-mysticism-and-christianity.php.

Chapter 4 – Telling "Your" Story

1. Matthew Henry, *Commentary on the Whole Bible*, Volume VI, 2 Timothy 4, http://www.ccel.org/ccel/henry/mhc6.iiTim.v.html.

2. Matthew Henry, *Commentary on the Whole Bible*, Volume VI, 2 Timothy 4, http://www.ccel.org/ccel/henry/mhc6.iiTim.v.html.

3. J.C. Ryle, *Apostolic Fears,* http://www.biblebb.com/files/ryle/warn7.txt.

4. Sally Lloyd-Jones, *The Jesus Storybook Bible*, (Grand Rapids: Zondervan, 2007), 12.

5. Ibid., 30.

6. Ibid., 32.

7. Ibid., 36.

8. Ibid., 351.

9. Rob Bell, *Love Wins*, (New York: Harper Collins Publishers, 2011), 2.

10. Ibid., 170.

11. Ibid., 144.

12. Ibid., 144.

13. Bill Johnson, *When Heaven Invades Earth Expanded Edition*, (Destiny Image, Inc., 2013), 29.

14. Ibid., 87-88.

15. Ibid., 88.

16. Ibid., 88.

17. Monergism, *The Definition of the Council of Chalcedon,* http://www.monergism.com/definition-council-chalcedon-451-ad.

18. Roma Downey and Mark Burnett, *A Story of God and All of Us: A Novel Based on the Epic TV Miniseries "The Bible,"* (New York: FaithWords, 2013).

19. The Washington Post, *Actress Roma Downey on religion, faith*, February, 9, 2012, http://www.washingtonpost.com/local/actress-roma-downey-on-religion-faith-219/2012/02/09/gIQATJNT1Q_video.html

20. Sarah Pulliam Bailey, *Sally Lloyd-Jones, 'Jesus Storybook Bible' Author, Sells Over 1,000,000 Books*, December 12, 2013, http://www.huffingtonpost.com/2013/12/07/sally-lloyd-jones-jesus-storybook-bible_n_4377733.html.

21. From Wikipedia, *Rob Bell*, http://en.wikipedia.org/wiki/Rob_Bell.

22. Bill Johnson, *Bethel Store*, https://shop.ibethel.org/vendors/bill-johnson-ministries.

23. THR staff, *Mark Burnett's 'The Bible' Becomes Top-Selling Miniseries on Blu-Ray and DVD*, April 8, 2013, http://www.hollywoodreporter.com/news/mark-burnetts-bible-becomes-top-434875.

24. John MacArthur, *The MacArthur Bible Commentary*, (Nashville: Thomas Nelson, 2005), 1813.

25. Charles Spurgeon, *Christ—The Power and Wisdom of God*, Sermon #132, delivered on Sabbath Morning, May 17, 1857, http://www.spurgeon.org/sermons/0132.htm.

26. Matthew Henry, *Commentary on the Whole Bible*, Volume VI (Acts to Revelation)," Christian Classics Ethereal Library, http://www.ccel.org/ccel/henry/mhc6.Col.iii.html.

27. John MacArthur, *The MacArthur Study Bible, New American Standard Bible Updated Edition,* (Nelson Bibles, A Division of Thomas Nelson Publishers, 2006), p 1747.

28. Robert H. Schuller, *Self Esteem: The New Reformation*, (Word Books, 1982), 67.

29. Guthrie, Motyer, Stibbs, Wiseman, *The New Bible Commentary: Revised (1970, Book Revised)*, (Wm. B. Eerdmans Publishing Co., 1984), 1254.

30. Michael Horton, *In the Face of God*, (Dallas: Word Publishing, 1996), 124.

31. Ibid., 124.

Chapter 5 – A Framework of Self

1. Steve Lawson, *The Heroic Boldness of Martin Luther*, (Reformation Trust Publishing: A Division of Ligonier Ministries, 2013), 120.

2. R.C. Sproul, *Ligonier Ministries Newsletter*, May 19, 2014.

3. Stephen Charnock, *The Existence and Attributes of God*, Vol. 1, (First reprinted 1979 by Baker Book House Company from the 1853 edition by Robert Carter and Brothers, Eleventh printing, May 1993), 240 & 241.

4. Bob DeWaay, *Redefining Christianity*, (Springfield, MO: 21st Century Press, 2006), 184.

5. Gary Gilley, *This Little Church Went to Market*, (Fairfax: Xulon Press, 2002), 23.

6. John MacArthur, *Reckless Faith*, (Wheaton: Crossway Books, 1994), 52-53.

7. Oswald Chambers, *The Psychology of Redemption*, (Oswald Chambers Publications Association, 1922; Second Edition, 1930, Third Edition, 1935), 68-70.

8. Charles Spurgeon, *Harvest Joy,* Sermon 2265, http://www.spurgeon.org/sermons/2265.htm.

9. *Merriam-Webster's Dictionary*, http://www.merriam-webster.com/dictionary/paradigm.

Chapter 6 – Disguised Redirection

1. Charles Spurgeon, *Satanic Hindrances*, A Sermon Delivered on Sunday Morning, October 29, 1865, at the Metropolitan Tabernacle, Newington. https://answersingenesis.org/education/spurgeon-sermons/657-satanic-hindrances/.

2. John MacArthur, *MacArthur Study Bible*, (Thomas Nelson, 2006), 958.

3. Steven Riser, *Deception: Discerning the Devil's Most Dangerous Device*, 2005, 1.7 Why Was Eve Deceived?, 3.

4. Sinclair Ferguson, *Medieval Mistakes*, (Founders Journal, Winter 2002), 27-29, http://www.founders.org/journal/fj47/article3.html.

5. Rick Warren, 40 Days of Purpose®, *The Purpose Driven® Life*, (Grand Rapids, Michigan: Zondervan, 2002); *40 Days of Purpose: Small Group & Sunday School Video Curriculum.*

6. Bob DeWaay, *Redefining Christianity: Understanding the Purpose Driven Movement*, (Springfield: 21st Century Press, 2006), 17.

7. Gary Gilley, *This Little Church Went to Market*, (Fairfax: Xulon Press, 2002), 74.

8. *Westminster Shorter Catechism* (1674), http://www.ccel.org/creeds/westminster-shorter-cat.html.

9. Harry L. Reeder, *Cultural Narcissism and a Titanic Lesson,* (Tabletalk Magazine: Ligonier Ministries Inc., March 2012), 8.

10. John MacArthur, *The Truth War,* (Nashville: Thomas Nelson, 2007), 197.

Chapter 7 – Falling Away Foretold

1. John Owen, *Nature and Causes of Apostasy from the Gospel*, http://www.ccel.org/ccel/owen/apostasy.i.vii.html#i.vii-p14.3.

2. John Calvin, *Commentary on Philippians, Colossians, and Thessalonians*, (Grand Rapids, MI: Christian Classics Ethereal Library, 1999-11-24, v1.0, URL 1999-11-24), http://www.ccel.org/ccel/calvin/comment3/comm_vol42/htm/vii.iv .htm.

3. Charles Spurgeon, *Comfort and Constancy, Sermon on 2 Thessalonians 2:16,17,* Sermon #2363, delivered on March 15, 1888 at Metropolitan Tabernacle, Newington, England.

4. Charles Spurgeon, *Pride the Destroyer*, Sermon #2591, 1898.

5. Matthew Henry, *Matthew Henry Commentary on 2 Thessalonians 2*, http://www.biblestudytools.com/commentaries/matthew-henry-complete/2-thessalonians/2.html.

6. John Calvin, *Commentary on Philippians, Colossians, and Thessalonians*, (Grand Rapids, MI: Christian Classics Ethereal Library, 1999-11-24, v1.0, URL 1999-11-24), http://www.ccel.org/ccel/calvin/comment3/comm_vol42/htm/vii.iv .htm.

7. Thomas Manton, *The Complete Works of Thomas Manton*, Vol. 3, Solid Ground; 1st edition, (July 1, 2008), 50.

8. John Calvin, *Commentary on Philippians, Colossians, and Thessalonians*, (Grand Rapids, MI: Christian Classics Ethereal Library, 1999-11-24, v1.0, URL 1999-11-24), http://www.ccel.org/ccel/calvin/comment3/comm_vol42/htm/vii.iv .htm.

Chapter 8 – Two Distinct Cities

1. Martin Luther, as cited by Rev. John Ker, D.D., *Lectures on the*

History of Preaching, (A.C. Armstrong & Son, 1889), 155.

2. Martin Luther, *Luther's Works, Vol. 51,* 388.

3. Horatius Bonar, Taken from *Light & Truth: Bible Thoughts & Themes*, Vol. V, 1872.

Made in the USA
Middletown, DE
08 November 2015